PALM BEACH

An Architectural Heritage

PALM BEACH

Stories in Preservation and Architecture

An Architectural Heritage

Shellie Labell, Amanda Skier, and Katherine Jacob
Foreword by Lady Henrietta Spencer-Churchill
Principal Photography by Stephen Leek

PRESERVATION
FOUNDATION
OF PALM BEACH

RIZZOLI
NEW YORK

New York · Paris · London · Milan

First published in the United States of America in 2018 by
RIZZOLI INTERNATIONAL PUBLICATIONS, INC.
300 Park Avenue South, New York, NY 10010
www.rizzoliusa.com

ISBN: 978-0-8478-6281-8
Library of Congress Control Number: 2018940290

"The Beginnings" (pages 14–29) was originally published in 2003 in
Palm Beach: An Architectural Legacy by Polly Anne Earl;
the essay as it appears in this book has been significantly revised
and expanded by the authors.

Photography acknowledgments appear on page 251.

Distributed to the U.S. Trade by Random House, New York

Endpapers: Ivor House, mural detail (see p. 242)
Page 1: Casa della Porta del Paradiso, ceiling detail (see p. 58)
Pages 2–3: Pelican House (see p. 214)
Pages 4–5: Pelican Hall, interior (see p. 206)
Pages 6–7: Las Campanas (see p. 130)
Page 11: South Lake Trail House, garden (see p. 92)
Pages 14–15: View from Casa de Leoni (see p. 74)

Designed by Abigail Sturges

Printed and bound in China

2018 2019 2020 2021 2022 / 10 9 8 7 6 5 4 3 2 1

CONTENTS

FOREWORD
Lady Henrietta Spencer-Churchill
10

PREFACE
12

THE BEGINNINGS
Polly Anne Earl
14

THE HOUSES
30

FOREWORD

Lady Henrietta Spencer-Churchill

The preservation of our historic homes and their rich history is vitally important, not only for future generations to appreciate, but also for us all to understand how our environment and social history have evolved, knowing they will continue to do so at an ever more rapid pace, potentially eradicating evidence of the past. There is a dilemma regarding the restoration or rehabilitation of historic and landmarked buildings. Do you restore a building to its original period and detail, or do you allow it to evolve to accommodate the change in building techniques, technology, and modern lifestyles?

Previous owners of an historic home may have already eradicated vital original architectural details. In these cases, you can only do your best to preserve what is worth keeping, or restore the building to its original appearance and style. Having been fortunate enough to grow up living in and participating in the restoration of many landmarked historic houses, I have realized that it is possible to be sympathetic to the architectural fabric of the building whilst modernizing it into the twenty-first century.

In the United Kingdom, and increasingly in the United States of America, local planning authorities and organisations may ultimately dictate which modifications to an historic structure are permitted, and can often heavily govern the process. It is easy to look at these restrictions with disdain, having potentially curbed your ambitious plans. Yet ultimately, we should be grateful for their presence and professional guidance in the process.

Successive governments and organisations have recognised that private owners remain the most economic and effective guardians of these properties. The owners bring a personal and passionate commitment to keeping the houses alive, and have a direct interest in their long-term survival. Governmental bodies in all nations need to do more to give support and tax relief in order to encourage long-term commitment. The historic environment is valued for its contribution to our knowledge and sense of identity, and because it helps to make places feel worthy. Participating in heritage-based projects can contribute to personal development and have a positive effect on health and wellbeing. The same can apply to public buildings. Concentrations of historic buildings add value to areas because they provide variation, human scale, and a connection to the past that visitors and residents alike can appreciate.

In historic Palm Beach, where my family has strong ties, it is wonderful to see the Preservation Foundation of Palm Beach carrying out such vital work in preserving the homes and legacies of so many important architects and families from the early twentieth century. The area has been forever transformed by the likes of Addison Mizner, Maurice Fatio, Marion Sims Wyeth, John Volk, and many other talented architects. Combining Italianate Mediterranean, Spanish, and Moorish-Gothic styles, these architects and builders created grand houses for the "new aristocracy" of the Gilded Age who wished to escape the cold harsh winters in the north. Coupled with its beautiful coastal setting, the Town of Palm Beach soon became a popular place to be seen and entertain during the social season.

The Town of Palm Beach was incorporated in 1911. In 1979, the Landmarks Preservation Commission was formed to create landmark designation criteria to protect historic buildings. The town now has over three hundred landmarked properties.

The Preservation Foundation of Palm Beach, a non-profit charitable foundation, was established in 1980 to educate people of all ages on the importance of preserving threatened buildings while ensuring that restorations are carried out in an appropriate manner. The Foundation has, through the generosity of many local donors, helped to successfully restore many local landmarks such as Sea Gull Cottage and the Town Hall. I am therefore delighted to support the Ballinger Award and endorse this latest volume of works illustrating the best restoration projects carried out in Palm Beach, and look forward to many more in the future.

Henrietta Spencer-Churchill

PREFACE

The Ballinger Award was named for the late Robert I. Ballinger, Jr., a forceful advocate for preservation and an early chairman of the Town of Palm Beach Landmarks Commission. Ballinger was born and educated in Philadelphia, graduated from Cornell's School of Architecture, and returned to Philadelphia to practice in The Ballinger Company, an architecture and engineering firm. Ballinger was particularly interested in and known for his work designing and renovating hospitals. He was a member as well as Chairman of the Landmarks Preservation Commission from 1979 to 1985. He was a knowledgeable preservationist and his architectural training and wisdom were invaluable.

The award is a silver medal designed by the noted sculptor, Edward R. Grove, whose work is in the Metropolitan Museum of Art, the Carnegie Institute, and the Smithsonian Institute. Grove is also the sculptor of the bicentennial eagle at the western end of Royal Poinciana Way in Palm Beach. In designing the Ballinger Medal, Grove worked from a sculpted head of Robert Ballinger created by his wife, Didi Ballinger.

The predecessor to this work, *Palm Beach: An Architectural Legacy*, was written by the late Polly Anne Earl, long-time Executive Director of the Preservation Foundation. Her other publications included articles, reviews, and a book on vintage postcards, titled *Palm Beach: The Way We Were.*

Creating a book is much like restoring a building: no detail is too small to ignore. These stories would have been impossible to compile without the diligent support of the Preservation Foundation staff.

The Preservation Foundation would like to thank the generous underwriters who made the book possible:

GRAND BENEFACTORS
The Honorable and Mrs. Wilbur L. Ross, Jr.

BENEFACTORS
The Honorable Mary M. Ourisman
The Price Family Foundation
St. Edward Catholic Church

Finally, the Preservation Foundation wishes to thank the many Palm Beachers who support our organization and mission. Their contributions have laid the foundation necessary to create this book. The authors would like to thank the Trustees and the Executive Committee of the Preservation Foundation for their dedication to Palm Beach's achitectural and cultural heritage.

THE BEGINNIN

In 1893, when Henry Flagler first came to Palm Beach, the town was still in the process of inventing itself. What had been a quiet settlement of pioneers and genteel sportsmen was galvanized into a hotbed of resort development by the impact of Flagler's Florida East Coast Railway and his destination hotels. The town never looked back as it went on to become, by the turn-of-the-century, an American Riviera without parallel in its wealthy clientele, its reputation for extraordinary entertainment and shopping, and, most of all, its endowment of glorious architecture. Flagler already had what is known today as a "business plan" for the profitable development of the east coast of Florida. With each extension of his railroad, Flagler, a former Rockefeller partner in the Standard Oil Company, also financed the building of a major hotel. St. Augustine, the terminus of the railway in 1890, required three hotels: the Ponce de Leon (1888), the Cordova, and the Alcazar (1889). They were hotels of distinction and immediately garnered round-trip business for the railway.

The next major terminus for the march down the East Coast was a matter of considerable interest to Florida's early settlers, who watched the same process on the West Coast as Henry B. Plant extended his railroad, the Southern Express Company, on the opposite side of the state. In Flagler's case, his selection of the hitherto unremarkable barrier island of Palm Beach may have been influenced from the start by Palm Beach's architecture. A tidbit of oral history speaks of an itinerant photographer who showed Flagler photographs of a Palm Beach house in the late 1880s. This house became Flagler's first home in Palm Beach. Ultimately it was known as Sea Gull Cottage. On seeing the photographs Flagler supposedly said, "Why I didn't know there was anything south of Rockledge as beautiful as that."

How Palm Beach attracted the interest of Henry M. Flagler, one of the authentic Gilded Age pioneers of America's great industrial revolution is the story of the beginning of Palm Beach as an international resort. Palm Beach was an unnamed wilderness on Florida maps in 1870, although Jupiter Inlet just to the north, with its 1860 Civil War lighthouse, was already named. In 1873 the first formal homestead in the Palm Beach area was filed by L. L. Hammond.

In 1878 the brig, *Providencia*, wrecked off the coast with a cargo of twenty thousand coconuts. The stranded brig provided Palm Beach's first agricultural craze when Hiram Hammon and William Lanehart, two early settlers, bought the cargo and resold it for 2.5¢ a coconut. Through this fortuitous circumstance Palm Beach acquired the fringe of coconut palms that gave it its name.

The Dimick, Gere, and Brown families from Michigan, who all played a role in the subsequent creation of a true community in Palm Beach, settled on the lakefront in 1876. Elisha N. "Cap" Dimick, expanded his lakefront home by eight rooms and opened it to winter visitors as the area's first hotel, the Cocoanut Grove House. In 1884 the Brelsford brothers, Edmund and John, established the first general store, which later also served as a post office. In 1885, the "barefoot mailman" legend began when local residents were hired to walk the beachfront delivering mail from Jupiter to Miami. For five dollars travelers who sought the comfort of an experienced guide could walk along with the mailman. The only alternative at the time was an ocean passage by sail, as there were no interior roads.

The year 1886 marked a turning point for Palm Beach. The community joined together to support its first school, a one-room venture that welcomed Hattie Gale, a sixteen-year-old, as its first teacher. Ladies held bake sales to raise money for the school, while the men contributed their labor for its construction. Once completed the school also became the center of pioneer religious life with the Congregationalists holding services there in the morning and the Episcopalians in the afternoon.

This one-room schoolhouse was the first school in southeast Florida. Palm Beach and Dade counties were not formally separated until 1909. Today the Preservation Foundation of Palm Beach operates a living history program for fourth graders in the original one room school. It is one of only about two dozen educational programs still operating in one-room schools throughout the entire United States. The one room school, now moved from its original lakefront location, has become affectionately known as the Little Red Schoolhouse.

The same year, R. R. McCormick of Denver, Colorado, built the house that became known as Sea Gull Cottage, the oldest extant home in Palm Beach. In many ways Sea Gull's history mir-

rors the development of the town. In a community of hunters, farmers, fishers, and trappers, Sea Gull Cottage, then known as the McCormick Cottage, a substantial Shingle style structure with a third-story tower, was acknowledged as the "showplace of the lake." McCormick could afford to endow his wilderness cottage with all the fine interior and exterior amenities that Victorians valued as he had recently retired from extensive business interests in Colorado.

Historical records are not clear as to why McCormick left Denver. Apparently, a fishing trip brought him to south Florida. What is clear is that with McCormick's purchase of the Albert Gere's lake-to-ocean site of fifty-two acres on the island of Palm Beach, the Denver railroad promoter and real estate entrepreneur inaugurated the cycle of ever increasing real estate prices that has characterized land in Palm Beach ever since. Gere had paid 85¢ an acre for his tract. McCormick bought it for a total of ten thousand dollars. It was the largest land transaction up to that time in the community and the wonder of local citizens who quite rightly surmised that even greater profits lay ahead for astute real estate investors.

For his ten thousand dollars McCormick got what he referred to as "truly a paradise." In the words of the previous owners, "the sky was bluer, the water clearer, the flowers sweeter, the song of birds more musical than could be found elsewhere on the continent . . . [Providence provided] sweet potatoes weighing ten and twelve pounds . . . forty pound watermelons . . . as well as eleven pound pineapples . . . the choicest fish, the best flavored venison, the tenderest bear steak . . . was ours, if we would but help ourselves . . . not to mention the generosity of the waves," which carried in all manner of goods, necessary and luxurious, from lard, to clothing, to iron cook-stoves. Balanced against these delights of nature and climate were the difficulties of insects, hurricanes, and remoteness. No doctor, minister, mortician, or school teacher resided on Lake Worth's shores at the time of McCormick's coming. Mailmen still walked the beaches and more than one pioneer gave up his stake and headed elsewhere because of the lack of regular transport. The all-water transport of the time precluded any effective marketing of cash crops.

Small wonder local descriptions of the McCormick place marvel over its hundreds of "magnificent and rare plants . . . beautiful promenades . . . redolent with the perfume of flaming tropic flowers." To the twenty thousand coconuts from the *Providencia* wreck and six hundred tropical trees of twenty-six varieties planted by the Geres, McCormick added seven hundred roses and two hundred chickens of "Fancy breeds." Visitors spoke of McCormick's horticultural efforts as, in reality, "a private experiment station" with two acres of clear area bordering the lake and "colonnades – of cocoanuts . . . flower-beds . . . containing fancy-leaved caladiums . . . and a bed of crotons, the finest private collection . . . ever seen," as well as lime, lemons, orange, sour-sop, sapodilla, tamarind, mango, date, and alligator pear (avocado) trees, pineapples and for vegetables, peas, lettuce, tomatoes, squashes, and cucumbers completing the fifty-two acres of the estate.

Commentators waxed even more rhapsodic over McCormick's house as "the crowning glory" of his estate. McCormick had moved rapidly to demolish the one and one-half story Gere House. Building materials were quickly imported on the first scheduled packet line on Lake Worth, via the schooner *Emily B.* Local recollection was proved correct when during the restoration of Sea Gull, boards were found in the walls marked for "R.R. McCormick, Lake Worth." Apparently even a former Denver millionaire was not above adopting local customs and profiting from the bounty of the sea, for Sea Gull's still magnificent mahogany staircase is said to have been constructed from lumber scavenged from the beach after a shipwreck. The local press noted other aspects of the house such as its "cool, well-ventilated rooms . . . fancy ornamental woods . . . and floors of Georgia marble. Handsome mirrors and furnishing impart a luxurious appearance . . . and a tower affords one of the most beautiful views of the surroundings." At a reputed cost of thirty thousand dollars McCormick's home commanded considerable local interest. The completion of such an up-to-date home signaled the beginning of the end of Palm Beach's pioneer days. Efforts to establish regular lake and ocean transport lines pointed toward the development of a stable cash economy and an influx of new residents.

By 1893, Flagler had completed his deliberations and purchased the land necessary for his railroad connections. Once again, the McCormick property figured prominently in the history of Palm Beach's development. Flagler's purchase of the McCormick property in 1893 for seventy-five thousand dollars gave him the location he needed for the Royal Poinciana Hotel, which was to be the largest wooden resort in the world.

Opening in 1895, the Royal Poinciana became a magnet for the rich and famous who could enjoy the social life afforded through the hotel, as well as the outdoor swimming, bicycling, fishing, and hunting offered by the Florida climate. McCormick's house, now Flagler's home, stood at the center of all activities. Its original location placed it at the very forefront of the hotel, between the hotel and the lakeside. During his winter sojourns in Palm Beach, Henry Flagler himself occupied the house. It was his first Palm Beach home and became known as "a house with two fronts and no back doors," probably from its proximity to the pedestrian traffic along the lakefront to the west and the bustle of traffic to and from the hotel on its east side. At this time, it acquired the name Croton Cottage, perhaps for the magnificent croton beds that McCormick had planted.

By the 1890s, McCormick's cottage had already served as the stylistic harbinger for a clutch of similar homes along Palm Beach's lakefront. All were built to accommodate the families of wealthy northerners who brought with them, as McCormick had, an architectural preference for high Victorian taste from the style centers of the north. Sea Gull's Shingle style, a popular architectural motif of the great Newport resort homes of the era, suited Florida well. Broad porches and high ceilings cooled the Florida heat. Towers or cupolas provided inviting views. An emphasis on wood as the primary construction material utilized the resources of the area.

As the earliest fine house in the area, Sea Gull no doubt provided a design source for many of the frame homes built in the 1890s, which formed the nucleus of Palm Beach's "cottage colony." Modern redevelopment, and a continuing admiration of Addison Mizner's Mediterranean Revival style has obscured the significance of the Shingle style in Palm Beach's architectural history. But it can be truly said that Palm Beach's earliest domestic architecture was typically American.

After Flagler purchased Sea Gull's lake-to-ocean tract of land, the Royal Poinciana Hotel was constructed around the cottage. The Royal Poinciana included over eleven hundred hotel rooms, fifteen hundred employees, and thirteen miles of corridors. The main dining room could hold over sixteen hundred diners at one time, and the ballroom was the scene every year of the Washington's Birthday Ball, the major event of the Palm Beach social season. In 1896, Flagler constructed the Palm Beach Inn, renamed The Breakers Hotel in 1901, on the oceanfront. The hotel burned to the ground in 1903, and again in 1925, and was rebuilt in fire resistant stucco from an Italianate design by the New York architects Schultze & Weaver.

Hotel guests at both hotels could avail themselves of The Breakers' ocean fishing pier where steamboats made the trip to Havana. They could golf and play tennis and watch the boat parades on Lake Worth. They could bicycle or stroll along Lake Trail, which remains today a pedestrian byway along Lake Worth, to visit the local attraction of Alligator Joe's, which displayed alligators and manatees in a jungle setting. New York stores were available for shopping at both hotels. Guests could travel down the pine walk between the hotels by a railcar drawn by a mule named Molly. Perhaps the most popular pastime of all was the afternoon tea dance at the Royal Poinciana's Cocoanut Grove where coconut cake was the dessert of choice.

The success of Flagler's hotels gave rise to the great era of hotels in Palm Beach. By the Roaring Twenties, America's economic prosperity, coupled with the vibrant Florida land boom had changed Palm Beach into a major resort with a hotel-based economy. The Alba (later named the Biltmore) was built during

The original dining room of Sea Gull Cottage was restored as a music room. The windows were reproduced from historic photographs.

OPPOSITE *The restored parlor of Sea Gull Cottage.*

22

The afternoon tea dance at the Royal Poinciana Hotel's Cocoanut Grove was a popular social event for all ages.

BELOW *This view of Sea Gull's Cottage parlor showcases the original marble floors and mahogany staircase present during R.R. McCormick's ownership from 1886 to 1893.*

OPPOSITE
LEFT AND RIGHT *In 1984, the Preservation Foundation moved Sea Gull Cottage back to its original lakefront orientation, approximately two blocks south of its original location. The moving process involved cutting the house in half. Once at its new location, the extensive restoration process could begin.*

this period, as were the Palm Beach Hotel, The Vineta Hotel, The Billows, and The Brazilian Court. An early railroad-only bridge was modified to provide auto access to the island. As a result, the northern commercial area of Palm Beach exploded with development. The Fashion Beaux Arts, a lakefront shopping area erected in 1917, was said to be the earliest shopping mall in America and featured a popular rooftop movie theater.

The hotel boom also provided a catalyst for entrepreneurs to create a residential infrastructure. In the early twentieth century, subdivisions were planned and interior streets began to be dotted with speculative houses, often in the then popular Bungalow style or in a Mission influenced variant of the American foursquare house. Developers provided a complete range of housing services, from auctions of raw land ready for construction, to rentals of fully furnished and staffed cottages. With the growth of the residential community, demand grew for amusements outside the hotels. Colonel E.R. Bradley opened Bradley's Beach Club, an elegant gambling and dining establishment in 1898.

In 1918, when Singer sewing machine heir Paris Singer, with architect Addison Mizner, opened the Everglades Club, Palm Beach became captivated by Mizner's theatrical Mediterranean Revival architecture which seemed to express the romance and opulence of the times. Singer distanced his development of the Everglades Club and Worth Avenue from Flagler's earlier enterprises with a single depreciating remark.

When asked what color he wanted to paint the club he is said to have answered, "anything but that damn yellow," referring to Flagler's liberal use of a color that sometimes appeared close to railroad switching engine yellow. Along with his appealing architectural designs, Mizner's promotional talents and gregarious personality made him the architect of choice for many of Palm Beach's great mansion builders.

The vogue for extravagant mansions culminated with the construction of Mar-a-Lago for Marjorie Merriweather Post Hutton, which began in 1923. The estate occupied seventeen acres and included fifty-eight rooms. Mar-a-Lago was a collaboration between Joseph Urban and Marion Sims Wyeth, both local architects of note. By 1927, Mizner had largely transferred the focus of his attention to his ill-fated development of the city of Boca Raton. Mizner's list of projects in 1926 includes only one house in Palm Beach. Mizner established the Mizner Development Company in 1925 to create, in Boca Raton, "the world's most beautiful architectural playground." But with the collapse of the wondrous Florida boom in real estate, influential backers like T. Coleman du Pont disassociated themselves from Mizner's firm. In Palm Beach, Mizner's legacy of astounding homes and the rise of Worth Avenue as one of America's international fashion and shopping meccas provided an enduring foundation for Mizner's reputation as a founding father of Palm Beach's architectural importance.

A view of Worth Avenue in the 1920s shows Villa Mizner's five story apartment overlooking the Town of Palm Beach.

Palm Beach's hotel era was supported throughout the 1920s by the popularity of the automobile. A rising middle class also found resort accommodations in more modest residential rooming houses on Palm Beach's interior streets. The town offered the enormous appeal of its character and its streets – a built environment without parallel in its architectural presentation. Sea Gull Cottage became a part of the hotel age when it was moved to the oceanfront in 1913 and became one of The Breaker's rental cottages. For seventy years the cottage that had been the pride of the early lakefront community served valiantly as a seasonal rental accommodating whole families and their staffs for the winter season.

In 1983, when the Preservation Foundation discovered Sea Gull was threatened with demolition as a result of The Breakers' plan to replace its cottages with new condominiums, protracted negotiations began to save Palm Beach's oldest house. An agreement was forged between The Breakers, the Preservation Foundation, and the Royal Poinciana Chapel, the interdenominational house of worship founded by Henry Flagler (ca. 1895), to move Sea Gull Cottage to the chapel's grounds. The Preservation Foundation agreed to restore Sea Gull as an adaptive restoration to serve the needs of the chapel and its own needs for a library. Sea Gull, which had been an active presence in the early development of Palm Beach and in the hotel era, thus played a continuing role as Palm Beach entered a new stage of preserving its architectural heritage.

Restoration consultants found that in its original interior appointments and embellishments, Sea Gull Cottage yielded to none in its portrayal of high style decorative taste for its time. The period photographs Henry Flagler saw showed a parlor with a fashionable gilt-patterned ceiling, perhaps a gilt leather, numerous Victorian wallpaper borders, handsome wood accents, and sparkling chandeliers. Of note were the vertical strips of molding that divided the wallpaper into sections. This may have been a decorator's touch from a high style center like Philadelphia or New York.

The prosperity of the hotel era also saw the final definition of the Town of Palm Beach with the completion of its outstanding civic center. Town Hall Square, today a landmarked historic district, is dominated by the Harvey and Clarke-designed Town Hall. Town Hall Square was completed in 1929 with Mizner's contribution of a monumental fountain, reminiscent, according to the late Dr. Donald W. Curl, Mizner's foremost architectural biographer, of an historic fountain in Madrid.

The completion of the major buildings in Town Hall Square also marked Palm Beach's first explicit self-recognition of its own architectural character and heritage. In 1929 the Garden Club of Palm Beach published its influential *Plan of Palm Beach*, which called for gracious arcades in the Town Square as well as other far-sighted refinements. The Arts Jury was established the same year, numbering the architects Addison Mizner, Marion Sims Wyeth, and John Volk among its members. This civic body was a forerunner of the town's present Architectural Review Commission.

The great expectations of the Boom Times were conclusively ended by the 1929 stock market crash and the subdued years of the Great Depression. Palm Beach had established itself as a leading American resort and its development continued but without some of the magnificent excesses of the earlier era. In the 1970s and 1980s, when the Town of Palm Beach became concerned about its disappearing heritage of historic architecture, Town Hall Square became an area of major interest.

The Preservation Foundation of Palm Beach has played a vital role in many projects that have enhanced the picturesque

The Fashion Beaux Arts, designed in 1917 by August Geiger, was reputed to be the first shopping mall in America.

nature of Palm Beach. Town Hall had lost its imposing tower in a hurricane, and the formerly open central motor court had been filled in with a mid-sixties addition of administrative offices by architect John Volk. The building had been painted an unrelenting chalk white and festooned with numerous projecting window air conditioners and conduits for electrical and telephone cables. Windows had been blocked with concrete.

The 1989 restoration of Town Hall focused public attention on the significance of restoration in renewing the vitality and usefulness of historic architecture. The project was funded by the Preservation Foundation and included opening the blocked windows and restoring the lost tower and its cast stone decoration. Details found on the original drawings which had never been built were incorporated in the restoration. Arched windows long covered at the fire station end of the building were exposed.

In 2009, the Preservation Foundation helped fund a second renovation and restoration of Town Hall. More ambitious than the project in 1989, the interior space was entirely renovated. Town Council chambers were completed renovated, and

a new public entrance was added to the north façade of the building. The easternmost door has been converted into an entrance, with glass and ironwork reminiscent of the entrance on the southern façade.

Since its dedication in 1989, Earl E.T. Smith Park has been a proud landmark in Palm Beach and a noteworthy illustration of the Preservation Foundation's community-oriented goals. A beautiful tribute to Smith, a resident of Palm Beach for over 50 years, the park is an integral part of the area's historic charm. Located directly west of Town Hall, the park's charismatic architecture and lush landscaping provide a peaceful and tranquil escape for residents to truly enjoy. Smith was a respected civic and political leader whose government career was distinguished by appointments from four presidents. He served his country and community as US Ambassador to both Cuba and Switzerland, Mayor of Palm Beach, and as the first Chairman of the Preservation Foundation of Palm Beach.

Established by the Preservation Foundation in 1994, Pan's Garden is a privately maintained green space open to the public. Over three hundred plants native to Florida are showcased

Addison Mizner's 1929 World War I Memorial Foundation completed the design of the central island in the historic Town Hall Square.

RIGHT *The Palm Beach Town Hall is distinguished by its arched windows, decorative balustrades, and a variety of cast stone embellishments.*

through different areas representing highland and wetland environments. Since its inception, Pan's Garden has been home to numerous interdisciplinary educational programs designed to provide students with a glimpse into the wonders of plants and the importance of preserving the world's natural resources.

On December 12th, 2017, a ribbon cutting ceremony was held to celebrate the completion of the Preservation Foundation's latest project: the $2.7 million beautification of Bradley Park. The date marked the 158th birthday of Colonel E. R. Bradley, who gifted the waterfront land to the town for use as a park upon his death in 1946. Located at the northernmost entrance to the town, the locally designated park is now a gathering place and a source of pride for the community. The park's historic tea house was restored and a broken coral stone terrace constructed with a restored Artemis fountain at its center. Inside the tea house, interpretive panels were installed to educate residents and visitors on the history of Palm Beach.

Like the Ballinger Award winning houses whose stories follow, the projects of the Preservation Foundation illustrate the worthiness in preserving the rich architectural heritage of Palm Beach for the future.

THE HOUSES

WARDEN HOUSE

1988 Ballinger Award

In 1988, the Preservation Foundation of Palm Beach awarded Warden House one of two inaugural Ballinger Awards for the remarkable rehabilitation of the historic Warden House into a multi-family condominium. Warden House, completed in 1922, was designed by the eclectic Californian Addison Mizner, one of Palm Beach's most illustrious architects. After an apprenticeship under California architect Willis Polk, Mizner moved to Florida in 1918 to convalesce after a near-fatal beating by hitchhikers in New York. In Palm Beach, he found a new palette upon which to realize his fanciful architectural visions. Over the last century, Mizner has remained the architect most prominently identified with Palm Beach's unique style, Mediterranean Revival. The style, a combination of Spanish, Italian, and Moorish architectural influences, was embraced by Palm Beachers in the first decades of the twentieth century.

Cooper C. Lightbown, a young builder who relocated to Palm Beach from Washington, D.C., in 1912, was responsible for bringing Mizner's vision for Warden House to life. Lightbown worked closely with Mizner on most of his major commissions during the 1920s land boom, even while serving as mayor of Palm Beach from 1922–28. Originally built for industrialist William Gray Warden of the Pittsburgh Oil Company and Standard Oil, this oceanfront masterpiece occupied a prime location on North Ocean Boulevard. Warden and his wife were active members of Palm Beach society, participating in civic affairs and serving as president of the Gulf Stream Club.

Warden House is an excellent example of the Mediterranean Revival style, featuring a U-shaped plan with a central patio, stone columns, arches, and circular stairway. The estate exemplifies Mizner's signature combination of old world charm and new world modernity. In 1978, the Palm Beach Town Council determined that Warden House was too large and deteriorated to attract a single-family buyer. The following year, the developer was permitted to transform the crumbling mansion into a six-unit condominium.

Rehabilitation of an historic structure is a monumental task that involves altering the building while preserving character-defining features. The rehabilitation process allows structures of historical value to be sensitively modernized, allowing them to remain economically viable. The restoration architect's eye for detail and respect for Mizner's original vision made him the ideal steward. By the time rehabilitation was completed in 1981, only five percent of the interior had been altered. Three years later, Warden House was placed on the National Register of Historic Places, a testament to the authenticity of the restoration architect's ingenuity.

Warden House stairway with its decorative chandelier.

A living room space with tile mosaic and pecky cypress beamed ceiling.

BELOW *A second living room space with cast stone fireplace surround and stenciled coffered ceiling.*

OPPOSITE *Courtyard with centrally located fountain. The cloister seen at left speaks to Mizner's fascination with monastic architecture.*

BIENESTAR

1988 Ballinger Award

Wyeth's trademark courtyard plans feature open air balconies connecting the upper rooms.

The villa known as Bienestar, Spanish for "well-being," was erected in 1924, just a stone's throw away from Warden House. A romantic Mediterranean Revival villa, Bienestar was designed in 1924 by architect Marion Sims Wyeth. Wyeth arrived in Palm Beach in 1919 after studying at Princeton, the Ecole des Beaux-Arts in Paris, and completing his architectural apprenticeship in New York. One of the earliest master architects working in Palm Beach, Wyeth designed over one hundred homes for many of Palm Beach's most distinguished residents, including E.F. Hutton and his wife Marjorie Merriweather Post. Bienestar's first owner was Frederick S. Wheeler, chairman of the American Can Company, which in the early twentieth century produced half of American tin. Informally known as the "Tin Can Trust," the company was sued by the United States government for violating the Sherman Antitrust Act's prohibition on non-competitive practices in 1913. Despite a finding that the company was a monopoly, the case was dismissed in 1916.

Bienestar exemplifies Wyeth's best work in the Mediterranean Revival style. Like Wyeth's own residence, Tre Fontane, an ample courtyard unites the different areas of the house and includes Mediterranean Revival details of cast stone, wrought iron, and pecky cypress that decorate the interior and exterior façades. The contractor in charge of the original construction, Benjamin Hoffman, excelled in all building trades and earned the status of master builder. Described by surveyors as a "small pleasant house with a few touches of Spanish Renaissance ornament," Bienestar's Renaissance style balconies stand in stark contrast to the simplicity and symmetry of the front façade.

During the rehabilitation of Bienestar in 1985, the two-story single-family home was converted into a six-unit condominium villa. Each unit is unique, with owners enjoying improved courtyards and gardens. The villas created by the project preserve the original layout of the house around a central courtyard, one of the most integral characteristics of Wyeth's designs. This iconic villa has retained its original tile and wooden flooring, barrel tile roof, stucco exterior, and decorative details. The careful rehabilitation of Bienestar modified the house in such a way that its distinctive features have been carefully restored. In 1988, Bienestar was landmarked as a significant historical structure of the Town of Palm Beach.

Historic image of entrance from the Preservation Foundation of Palm Beach's Wyeth collection.

RIGHT *Modern day image of primary façade after restoration.*

MISSION HOUSE

1989 Ballinger Award

The aptly named Mission House was constructed in 1923 by master builder Benjamin Hoffman. Although Mission House was not landmarked and has since been demolished, the graceful Mission Revival style lakefront home was a testimony to the quality of architecture that became typical throughout the town during the Boom Times of the early 1920s. The house was built as a Mission influenced interpretation of the Spanish Revival style and was modified over the years.

A building permit from 1923 indicates that Mission House was built for Arthur D. Claflin of New York at a cost of $50,000, to be erected from stucco on hollow tile with a tile roof. Originally designed by Benjamin Hoffman, it underwent significant alterations by the architectural firm Wyeth, King, & Johnson in 1947, when it assumed a more modern form. Staff housing was added in 1952, and an addition in 1983 created a modern pool area. During the final restoration of Mission House in 1987, which added a new garage and apartment, many of the details from the original design were enhanced.

Key architectural features of Mission House included a three-story bell tower that lent a balancing effect to the home's two wings. Modern arches over the pool recognized the historical period of the home's construction. The tower's recessed arched windows and interior lent the house an ecclesiastical appearance, reminiscent of early Spanish Colonial missions.

Despite Mission House's historical significance and award-winning rehabilitation, the building's demolition in 1997 by a subsequent owner is a cautionary tale for preservationists. Designating a building as a landmark under the Town of Palm Beach's landmark ordinance is the only way to protect a building from demolition. As a result of the demolitions of Ballinger Award winning properties, the Preservation Foundation has determined that all future recipients must be landmarked homes to encourage not only the rehabilitation of historic properties, but to showcase the importance of the landmarks program.

A three-story bell tower was the focal point of this Mission-inspired residence.

VICARAGE

1990 Ballinger Award

Designed by Howard Major, two octagonal gazebos connected by a wall mark the lakefront limits of the Vicarage property. The two structures act as sentinels, both introducing and defining the lakefront location of the house and its lap pool.

Since its genesis in Florida's pioneer days, the Vicarage has undergone two major transformations, beginning as a simple wood-frame clapboard and shingle rectory, and later growing into a splendid two-story modern home. The Vicarage was built in the 1890s as a rectory for the vicar of the Bethesda-by-the-Sea Episcopal Church. A picturesque Moorish influenced shingle style structure, the Vicarage was constructed on Palm Beach's picturesque Lake Trail, which was the major artery of transportation on the island. Built before architectural records and permits were required, the architect and builders of the first incarnation of the Vicarage have been lost to history.

In Palm Beach, Howard Major is most frequently remembered as the architect of Major Alley, a charming pedestrian enclave of Bermuda style apartments built in the 1920s. Yet he also demonstrated his versatility by designing houses in many different architectural styles. Major's 1929 rehabilitation of the Vicarage blended the original vernacular style structure with a British West Indies design, adding a wing for bedrooms and staff quarters. He added distinctive lakefront octagonal gazebos and garden area, as well as the fanciful east entrance with a hint of Chinese influence.

Natural forces also contributed to the necessity of restoring the Vicarage. The disastrous Okeechobee hurricane in September 1928, which made landfall as a category four storm, decimated the Palm Beach area. Over twenty-five hundred people living near the Atlantic coast drowned in the storm surge, making it the second most deadly hurricane in the United States to date. In addition to the tragic loss of life, around two thousand homes and businesses on the island were destroyed or heavily damaged, including the church vicar's residence, which Major purchased and reconstructed the following year. Major took the Vicarage as his residence, where he lived until his death in 1974. His widow then sold the home to silent film actor Douglas Fairbanks, Jr., who used the Vicarage as both a residence as well as an entertainment hub for celebrities and royalty, including the Duke and Duchess of Windsor.

In 1989, the Vicarage underwent a major restoration. The restoration included a complete renovation of the interior, new windows, an updated façade, and enlarged rooms. A south side loggia was created during the restoration of the Vicarage, adorned with lush greenery. Designated as the town's first landmark property in 1979, the Vicarage has assumed many faces and has been intertwined not only with the town's architectural history but also with its social history since its pioneer-era beginnings over a century ago.

The fretwork-patterned portico was
added by Howard Major in 1929.

OPPOSITE. *The west façade, facing Lake
Worth, retains the original veranda while
the porch below has been enclosed to
increase living space.*

FIGULUS IV

1991 Ballinger Award

Figulus IV was a Shingle Style guest house inspired by one of Palm Beach's first oceanfront homes and one of four Palm Beach structures that have shared the name Figulus. The Ballinger Award Selection Committee departed from the award's restoration theme, bestowing the first and only award ever given to a new house. Since that time, the Elizabeth L. and John H. Schuler Award was established in 2005 to recognize new architecture reflective of Palm Beach's architectural traditions.

The first iteration of Figulus, Latin for "potter," was named in honor of the pioneering Potter family who first owned the land on which Figulus would be built. Figulus was erected in 1893 by Forrest Coburn of the Coburn & Barnum architectural firm and Palm Beach builder William Lainhart for the politically powerful Bingham family. Charles W. Bingham's father was an Ohio State Senator. His wife's father was also involved in politics, serving in the United States Senate. Charles and Mary's daughter Frances P. Bolton was later elected to the United States House of Representatives, and was the first woman from Ohio to serve in the United States Congress.

Figulus I was placed on the National Register of Historic Places in 1972, but was demolished in 1974 after a fire damaged it beyond repair. The Spanish Colonial style Figulus II, built adjacent to Figulus I in the 1920s, was also demolished near the turn of the twenty-first century. Figulus III and Figulus IV were both completed in 1989; Figulus III was the main house, with Figulus IV serving as the property's guest house. Designed as a family vacation cottage, Figulus IV was a welcoming home with an east-west orientation, high ceilings, broad porch, and informal plan capturing ocean breezes.

Figulus IV, conceived by Bingham family descendant Kenyon C. Bolton III, exemplified Palm Beach's pioneer Shingle style architecture. The front porch featured a variety of woodworking as showcased through the home's siding, balustrades, columns, and shutters. The Ballinger Award recognized Bolton's impressive accomplishment, demonstrating that new construction can recall the spirit of Palm Beach's past.

Prevalent during the pioneer era of Palm Beach, the Shingle Style was a simplified version of Victorian architecture.

EL SARMIENTO

1991 Ballinger Award

El Sarmiento was originally designed by Addison Mizner, but several Palm Beach architects have altered the house since its completion in 1923. The oceanfront residence began as a Mizner-designed courtyard home, yet what makes this house particularly notable is that it is one of the last surviving examples of Viennese architect Joseph Urban's works in Palm Beach. Completing his education in Vienna, Urban moved to the United States in 1911 and worked as a theatrical and art designer for the Boston Opera Company and the Metropolitan Opera in New York City. Urban's reputation led him to design the Ziegfeld Theater and the New School for Social Research, neither of which survive today.

The Mediterranean Revival gem was built for Anthony J. Drexel Biddle Jr. of the prominent Philadelphia banking family, who named the home after his grandmother, Jane Sarmiento. Biddle was the heir of an eccentric millionaire, with a penchant for boxing, and served as the United States Ambassador to Norway, Poland, the Netherlands, Yugoslavia, and Czechoslovakia.

Although the Palm Beach social season originally ended on George Washington's birthday in February, as the season became longer, later homeowners found the need for larger entertaining areas, more guest rooms, and additional housing for staff. In 1927, Urban created for El Sarmiento a grand oceanfront dining room for eighty people, complete with a stage for theatrical performances. A second addition by the prominent Palm Beach architectural firm Treanor & Fatio was added to the two-story home in 1936.

The loggia features restored ceilings, arches, and columns blended with modern art. The living room exemplifies skilled interior design through unification of the historic living space with a recently added Baroque-style painted wood ceiling. A new library features pecky cypress paneling. The award-winning rehabilitation of El Sarmiento was completed in 1989 after three years of work to restore the estate to the glory of its early days.

LEFT *The rounded end of Urban's addition to Mizner's 1923 residence houses a stage for theatrical performances.*

TOP *The living room features a decorated wood painted ceiling*

ABOVE *The stage end of Urban's dining room addition references its theatrical inspiration through black marble columns with intricately carved capitals.*

Mizner's original courtyard plan is an important feature of El Sarmiento. Urban's signature rejas can be seen on the second-floor patio.

BUTTONWOOD

1992 Ballinger Award

Buttonwood displays the fine tradition of frame vernacular style craftsmanship that characterized the earliest Palm Beach homes. Referred to as Orangerie until 1917, the house now known as Buttonwood was completed in 1905 for the mayor of Palm Beach, the Honorable E. N. "Cap" Dimick. After Dimick's death in 1917, his lake-to-ocean property became El Mirasol, the Mizner-designed Stotesbury estate.

In 1919, Orangerie quite literally "moved on" to become Buttonwood. Using hundreds of wooden rollers and a mule turning a capstan, the house was moved three blocks to the south and renamed Buttonwood after a magnificent buttonwood tree in the front yard. The home was then purchased by Amy Lyman Phillips, author of the popular 1920s *Palm Beach Post* society column "Diary of Mistress Samuel Peeps."

Typical of early Palm Beach architecture, Buttonwood's anonymous local builder worked in the familiar vernacular style that borrowed stylistic elements, such as Colonial columns and Queen Anne octagonal forms, from more traditional academic styles. Over the next several decades, Buttonwood endured many changes and additions. Its tower was lost, the octagonal second floor bedroom was squared off, and the interior appointments were changed.

By 1989, Buttonwood's wood frame was heavily damaged. Despite the amount of work needed to restore the house, it was purchased by Palm Beach newcomers who saw the unique beauty of the pre-Mizner era house. Rehabilitation of the historic home included installing new clapboard, custom milled to reproduce the exact dimensions of the historic siding, as well as custom beaded wainscoting in the halls and stairwell. Original columns, adding a simple elegance to the front porch, were split and reinforced before reinstallation. Despite Buttonwood's age, the home has retained many of its distinctive features, including a third-floor dormer on the front façade and the parlor wing's octagonal bay window. An octagonal conservatory wing added during the project mirrors the original parlor, reaching into the garden surrounding it. Buttonwood became a landmark in 2018.

Colorful tiles in a bathroom, along with a cane seat, recall Victorian era décor.

Buttonwood, when it was the Dimick home and known as Orangerie, was a typical frame vernacular Shingle Style home with the embellishment of a Queen Anne style tower.

RIGHT *The sprawling Buttonwood tree in the front yard gave the home its new name after it was moved from the Stotesbury property.*

CASA DELLA PORTA
DEL PARADISO

1993 Ballinger Award

Casa della Porta del Paradiso, or "House of the Door to Paradise," was designed by Swiss architect Maurice Fatio, who described it as the "greatest house [he had] ever done." While fellow architect Addison Mizner was introducing Spanish-influenced architecture in Palm Beach, Fatio was broadening his palette to encompass more Mediterranean sources by drawing on his knowledge of Italian architecture. Born into a wealthy banking family and having studied architecture at the Zürich Polytechnic, Fatio moved to New York City in 1920 to gain experience working with American architectural styles. In 1921, he formed a successful partnership with senior architect William A. Treanor; the pair followed their client base to Palm Beach four years later.

Casa della Porta was designed in 1928 for William McAneeny, then president of the Detroit-based Hudson Motor Car Company, the third largest automobile company in the nation at the time, manufacturing the "Hudson Twenty," one of the earliest affordable American automobiles. McAneeny moved in high circles, often hosting General George C. Marshall, then Secretary of State and Secretary of Defense. Casa della Porta was where a large portion of the Marshall Plan was conceived.

In comparison to many Palm Beach residences of the era, the building was small and the number of rooms limited, yet its beauty is expressed through its exquisite detail. Town and Country magazine noted Fatio's use of quarried keystone, a rare limestone from the Florida Keys, as well as the home's Romanesque and Florentine inspirations. The estate, inspired by Italian medieval monasteries, incorporated covered loggias, a cloistered stone courtyard, handcrafted ceiling details, and arched entryways.

The doorway of Casa della Porta appears the same as it did in 1929, with its splendid decoration of biblical motifs telling the story of Adam and Eve. The delicate carving is recorded to have taken six months for Italian stone carvers to complete. Whimsical, elegant, and sometimes grotesque carvings were resurrected through thousands of hours of laborious, detailed, and skilled restoration work by artisans. Majestic and monumental in its asymmetrical massing and intricate rooflines, Casa della Porta reflects the Tuscan influences that Fatio loved.

Fatio's contemporaries noted the home's state-of-the-art retractable windows that opened the house to the spacious patio, the windows descending into the basement. Many decades later during Casa della Porta's restoration, pieces of window mechanisms were found and carefully reassembled, restoring their original function throughout the house. The restoration of Casa della Porta was unlike many other award-winners, in that there was no new construction. Rather, the estate was meticulously restored to its original appearance, down to the most intricate detail.

The loggia leading from the tennis court to the central patio is decorated with an elaborate wooden ceiling. Decorated ceilings are a frequent theme throughout the house.

RIGHT The doorway of Casa della Porta is distinguished by its coquina stone decoration of biblical motifs. The coquina stone adds depth, color, and texture to the façade, while it unifies the asymmetrical Romanesque massing of the house. Differing window styles and cornice treatments add punctuation to the weight of the stone.

Casa della Porta's magnificent living room featured a hearth of truly noble proportions, flanked by gothic leaded glass windows.

During the restoration, when disassembled pieces of window mechanisms were found in the basement, they were painstakingly reassembled and reinstalled.

OPPOSITE The restoration preserves Fatio's ironwork. This stunning view highlights the original proportions of the stairway. The ceiling rises twenty-eight feet above the stair.

COLLADO HUECO

1994 Ballinger Award

Designed by Addison Mizner with a later addition by John Volk, Collado Hueco is a splendid example of the rare ability to strike the delicate balance between architectural design and location. The owners' goal for the house was to create "the look of centuries," accomplished through the skillful blending of new and old in the tradition of the outstanding architecture that has made Palm Beach famous for over a century.

Collado Hueco was designed for lawyer and businessman Paul Moore, the son of steel magnate W.H. "Judge" Moore of New York. Moore worked to consolidate his father's legacy following the "Great Merger Movement" era, when corporate interests clashed with United States antitrust law to prevent industrial monopolies.

The name Collado Hueco, or "hollow hill," combines the meanings of both prominence and declivity. The home's relationship with its hillside location is reflected in the contrast between its stucco surfaces and the natural coquina walls that seem to emerge from the earth itself. By building the house on the top of a natural ridge, Mizner preserved both ocean and lake views for the major rooms.

The design includes red clay barrel tile roofs, half timbering, and other elements that recall the organic materials and simple forms used in Mediterranean villages. Collado Hueco is unusual among Mizner's designs for its lack of applied cast stone decoration. Mizner's indoor-outdoor style was one of his specialties. The use of patios, loggias, and enclosed courtyards creates a distinctly Floridian setting.

Collado Hueco's rehabilitation was completed over a period of three years. Floors were removed, re-milled, and refinished, and worn tiles were restored and replaced where necessary. Mizner's original designs for the ceilings were painstakingly retraced and repainted. As an architect, the owner designed or reinterpreted many areas of the house, including the patio, east and west terraces, pool house and pavilion, French doors, and a terrace for the John Volk-designed guest house. Aside from adaptations to facilitate a modern lifestyle and the rehabilitation of Volk's guest house, the house remains as Addison Mizner designed it nearly a century ago. Collado Hueco was designated as an historic landmark by the Town of Palm Beach in 1980.

Intricate ironwork crowns a gazebo overlooking Lake Worth.

The massive front entrance arch shows Mizner's departure from his usual stucco construction. Here he used coquina stone for the first floor with half-timbering on the second level.

Viewed from the pool terrace, Collado Hueco recalls Mizner's philosophy of designing buildings to appear as though they grew organically over time.

The entrance hall features a Cuban tile
floor, simple wood balustrade, and a
substantial beamed ceiling.

BRAZILIAN BUNGALOW

1995 Ballinger Award

The award-winning Brazilian Bungalow was constructed for L.D. Cowling by East Coast Builders. Mrs. Cowling, who served as chairwoman of the Palm Beach County Suffrage Association, was active in the women's suffrage movement of the 1910s, even organizing a suffrage parade at the height of Palm Beach's social season. Designed and executed by anonymous craftsmen, Bungalow style houses occupied the cross streets in the center of the Town of Palm Beach. From 1905–25, the Bungalow style became the single most popular architectural style, both in Palm Beach and throughout the United States.

Conflicting sources place the build date between 1910–1925, a common occurrence before modern-day building codes were adopted in 1921. Since Palm Beach's bungalows tended to be one-story structures built on small lots, they were among the first of many casualties of demolition, the lots cleared to make room for the newer, larger homes increasingly in vogue during the Boom Times. Bungalows in Palm Beach tended to be much smaller than the mansions built by the town's notable architects, as they were built by local craftsmen and builders for middle class families. These low houses, with breezy front porches, dormer windows for light and air, bay windows, exposed roof beams and rafter tails, and broad eves, were conducive to Florida living. Many of the defining characteristics of the understated style, such as low-pitched, gabled roofs, full-width porches are represented in the Brazilian Bungalow.

This award-winning property retained its architectural integrity throughout the 1992 rehabilitation, respecting the typical elements of Bungalow style, while rehabilitating elements of the home to accommodate modern living. Additions were made to the rear façade of the house to expand the kitchen and a bedroom, and to frame a new pool and patio. The rear walls were pushed out and the roof lines were adapted to create a master bedroom suite upstairs as well as a dining and loggia area below. This Palm Beach home offers a modern take on the century-old Bungalow style.

Designated in 1995 as a landmark, the Brazilian Bungalow is typical of the charming early bungalows that formerly proliferated in Palm Beach. Yet this style is the town's most rapidly vanishing architectural style. This recipient of the 1995 Ballinger Award honored the hard work of faithfully rehabilitating an historically significant yet endangered architectural style. Inspired by the restoration of this modest home, the Polly Earl Award was established in 2005 to recognize property owners for the rehabilitation of smaller properties such as Brazilian Bungalow.

OPPOSITE *Distinctive in its high-pitched roof, this side-gabled bungalow is unusual. Most representations of the style feature low-pitched roofs and street facing gables.*

LEFT *A view of the living room looking toward a traditional window seat, added in the restoration, shows a simple wood window framed by the relaxed arch above the window seat and flanked by built-in bookcases.*

BELOW LEFT *A bay window expands the dining room, and the interior design repeats the arch motif found on the exterior. Reproductions of typical period windows were constructed with smaller lites in the top sash, forming a decorative element. The reconfiguration of the back of the house allowed the dining room to open toward the outdoor view.*

CASA DE LEONI

1995 Ballinger Award

The lakefront Casa de Leoni, located just west of the Everglades Club, is one of the best examples of Mizner's early work in Palm Beach. Although a departure from Mizner's usual Spanish style, Casa de Leoni's in-town location, small building site, and waterfront orientation blended with its surroundings and retained the essence of a Mizner villa. Named after its first owner, Casa de Leoni was commissioned in 1921 by Leonard Thomas of Philadelphia, a diplomat who had served as secretary of both the American legation in Madrid and the embassy in Rome. These experiences had a massive influence on Thomas, making Mizner an ideal architect for a Venetian style villa in Palm Beach.

Relying on the Venetian Gothic style to create a true Venetian villa at the edge of Lake Worth, Casa de Leoni rises directly out of the water on the east and south exposures, making it accessible both by land and water. Historians posit that Thomas' original plan included hiring Italian staff for Casa de Leoni, as well as importing Italian furniture and even a gondola, but this was never executed. Built of terra cotta structural tile with stucco cladding, Casa de Leoni's quarried keystone walk leads to an elaborate arched doorway at the land entrance, boasting a relief sculpture of the Lion of St. Mark above a paneled oak door. Mizner's creation included a large chimney with a dovecoat cantilevered on brackets, and trefoil-arched windows.

The water gate on the Lake Worth side of Casa de Leoni features two balustrades framing the boat landing. Several second story windows include balconies overlooking the water, and broad steps descend to the waterfront. An addition by Marion Sims Wyeth in the 1950s created a swimming pool and pool wing compatible with the original Mizner structure.

Casa de Leoni's exquisite rehabilitation was completed in 1992 by European craftsmen brought in for the project. The interior design was executed as a dramatic complement to Mizner's contrast of light and shade, heightening the romance of Mizner's vision. The home's decorative theme was based on details like the relief sculpture of the lion, which is represented throughout the house in wood, cast stone, tile, and brass hardware. Casa de Leoni was landmarked by the Town of Palm Beach in 1983, recognizing the historic and aesthetic value of Mizner's innovative approach to building an in-town house on a relatively limited site. It stands as a testament to Mizner's unique visions and demonstrates the value of restoring a classic structure to represent both the past and the present.

Casa de Leoni's restored entrance features the Lion of St. Mark.

FOLLOWING PAGES *Casa de Leoni's lakeside façade displays its typical Venetian water gate, an architectural feature that allowed visitors to arrive comfortably by boat.*

Vibrant patterns are a theme in a lake-side sitting room.

OPPOSITE *Casa de Leoni's living room, an incredible blending of texture, color, and pattern, with a remarkable stenciled ceiling, is a fitting stage for the glorious lake views outside.*

LEFT *The master bedroom features Moorish arches and gold egg-and-dart molding.*

ABOVE *Cast stone balustrades are an integral design feature on the lakeside.*

BETHESDA-BY-THE-SEA
EPISCOPAL CHURCH

1996 Ballinger Award

Bethesda-by-the-Sea, or "House of Healing by the Sea," has a long and storied history, its first incarnation dating back to 1886, when the congregation met in a frame vernacular building now known as the "Little Red Schoolhouse." Three years later, the congregation moved to its own building, also a simple wooden structure. By 1895, the church needed to expand to accommodate its growing congregation, and built a Moorish influenced church on the Lake Trail. After three decades, the congregation of Bethesda once again outgrew its facility, and sought to build a gothic cathedral in paradise.

The cornerstone of Bethesda's third and current iteration, including a tower nearly two hundred feet tall, was laid in 1925 by renowned New York architectural firm Hiss & Weekes. The firm is responsible for many of New York's Beaux-Arts style buildings, primarily apartments and hotels, a fine example of which was the Neoclassical style luxury Gotham Hotel, now the Peninsula New York, on 5th Avenue in New York City.

Bethesda's exquisite architectural detail welcomes parishioners at the main entrance with stone sculptures of the four apostles surrounding the door. A tympanum, or decorative area over the entrance bounded by a lintel and arches, shows the figure of Jesus Christ, represented holding a model of the church, his right hand raised in a blessing to all who enter. Above the high altar is a sapphire-colored *Te Deum* window, made in England in 1940 and sent to the United States in three separate ships for protection against attacks during the Second World War.

Many structural and aesthetic issues necessitated the restoration of Bethesda-by-the-Sea, beginning in 1994. In addition to nearly a century of use, the church's proximity to the salty Atlantic had corroded structural elements. Salt- and age-related deterioration included water damage on the outer walls, visibly rusted steel rebar, and cracked stone and mortar joints. To mitigate damage during the restoration, the restoration architects began with a "test wall" on which all chemicals and paints were subjected to trial and error analysis.

The church used state-of-the-art technology to protect forty-one precious stained-glass windows, now covered with a clear laminate that can withstand hurricane force winds. Two of these irreplaceable windows date from seventeenth-century Switzerland. Bethesda's restored details are exquisite, from its Della Robbia decorations, Madonnas, gargoyles, and arches, to its beautiful Tiffany window installed in an interior room.

The 1926 completion of Bethesda was made possible by the devotion and tenacity of its congregation. The Bethesda-by-the-Sea Episcopal Church, in all its incarnations, has remained a significant social and religious institution in Palm Beach for over a century. Its magnificent renovation reminds us of the spirit of restoration and preservation is not to remove the appearance of age, but rather only the damage.

View along the Gothic colonnade at the front of the church. The pillars illustrate the variety in color and size of the cast stone blocks.

OPPOSITE *The third Bethesda-by-the-Sea is dominated by its entrance tower.*

JUNGLEWOOD

1996 Ballinger Award

The rehabilitation of Junglewood was a labor of love for its owners, whose family lived in the house for generations. Designed by architect Julius Lee Jacobs of New York City in 1924 and completed three years later by contractor George W. Brown, Junglewood is one of three extant commissions by Jacobs in Palm Beach. In addition to executing his own designs, Jacobs served as Mizner's chief designer, running Mizner's office and supervising projects in his absence. Although almost nothing is known about Jacobs, his remaining works speak eloquently to his gifted eye for design.

Junglewood's first owner was Stanley Warrick, well-known in Palm Beach as early as 1916 and creator of the first shopping area in Palm Beach not owned by Henry Flagler, the Fashion Beaux Arts shopping center on the Lake Trail. Warrick was Palm Beach's entertainment pioneer of the 1920s, opening the first two movie theaters and the first nightclub on the island. The Warrick family was well known for hosting themed parties; their 1930 "Pajama Supper Dance" was attended by over fifty pajama-clad winter visitors happily dancing the night away, and their 1933 "Shipwreck Party" awarded prizes to the best and worst "shipwreck chic" costumed guests.

Representative of Warrick's theatrical interests, Jacobs designed a grand theatrical setting for Junglewood. It is unique in its unusual structural combination, with stucco on the first floor and half-timbering on the second. Described by contemporaries as "palatial," the house features a great tower, a winding staircase inlaid with colorful tile risers, and leaded glass windows. Junglewood's tiled doorway with a rope-pattern cast stone motif, a tiled Madonna and child plaque crowned by a cross, a monk's figure in cast stone, and decorative ironwork all show how Jacobs used every opportunity possible to integrate fascinating details into Junglewood.

The three-year rehabilitation of Junglewood enhanced the entrance to the pergola area with an arch and Spanish door, as well as other sensitive adjustments, including a new pool pavilion, and enhancements to the interior courtyard to complement the architectural integrity of the house. The original beamed ceilings and terra cotta tile floors were preserved during the process.

Further dramatic emphasis was added via refreshed landscaping, recognized with an Award of Excellence from the Florida Nurserymen and Growers Association. Junglewood's elaborate details, such as arches, pecky cypress, timbering, and asymmetric massing are demonstrative of Jacobs' dramatic flair and impressive talent. Although Jacobs was not a well-known architect in Palm Beach, the eight-bay Junglewood was designated as an historically significant landmark property in 1992, cementing his place in Palm Beach's illustrious history.

The grand stairway at Junglewood focuses on a colored glass leaded window with a cross motif. Jacobs employed many religious themes in Junglewood's decoration. Local newspapers also noted the stone stairway was intended to imitate travertine stone.

The dining room features two leaded glass
windows and paneling that terminates just
above the windows and arched doorway.

The spacious living room is defined by pillars with decorated capitals and an arched entrance. Details include a pecky cypress ceiling and stone fire-place. The Warricks, the original own-ers, were mentioned frequently in the Palm Beach newspapers as entertaining in grand style in their palatial home.

OPPOSITE *The pool pavilion designed by the restoration architect complements the historic architecture.*

ABOVE *A glimpse of the pool pavilion can be seen in the distance through the lush landscaping.*

SOUTH LAKE TRAIL HOUSE

1997 Ballinger Award

The dining room alcove provides space for an intimate dining area.

The 1938 Neoclassical style South Lake Trail House evokes Palm Beach's early pioneer years and epitomizes architect John Volk's dedication to simplicity and elegance. In 1880, Elisha N. "Cap" Dimick, the first mayor of Palm Beach, built the island's first hotel, named Cocoanut Grove, on the island's Lake Trail. Six months after the hotel was sold to Pittsburgh businessman Charles Clarke in the early 1890s, the hotel was destroyed by fire. Clarke then commissioned a house known as Primavera, the identity of its architect lost to time. Little is known about this late nineteenth-century home, but Primavera is believed to be one of Palm Beach's first non-wooden homes, adorned with white stucco exterior walls.

According to local lore, the frame of Primavera is rumored to be hidden within the walls of Volk's South Lake Trail House. Volk designed South Lake Trail House in 1938 for Charles S. Davis, president of the Borg Warner Corporation, an automotive components and parts supplier most famous for its role in developing the Studebaker's automatic transmission and a turbocharger for German automaker Porsche.

Complementing the unique ambiance of the location, the home's fine detailing and subtle, well-proportioned design worked together to create the splendid yet understated estate. With views of Lake Worth from nearly every room, Volk fulfilled Davis' request that every room "reflect the elegance of an English Manor house." The result was a combination of fine cornices, a grand Georgian style stairway, Adamesque woodwork details, an arched entrance flanked by tall windows, and an exposed chimney which breaks the horizontal line of the string course, denoting the second floor.

During the restoration of this fine estate, much care was taken to preserve Volk's classical detailing, and the home was restored in a refined Regency style that complements the mood of the tropics. South Lake Trail House is known for its splendid gardens, which Volk called "the most extensive in Palm Beach." Restoration of the gardens, including a ceiba tree brought from Nassau in the late nineteenth century by Clarke's son Louis, mirrored most of Volk's original design. A painstaking excavation of the original foundations recreated the garden's splendid reflecting pools and parterre plantings.

Designated as a landmark in 1990, the regal South Lake Trail House is deeply rooted in the history of Palm Beach. The restoration of the historic estate on the Lake Trail has maintained the character of Volk's vision for one of Palm Beach's earliest estates.

PREVIOUS PAGES
LEFT *The garden façade is one of the most distinguished elements of the South Lake Trail House. Classical arches on the first floor are offset by a string course and rectangular windows above. Mechanical equipment was concealed by strategically placed dormers on the third floor.*

RIGHT *The garden vistas feature an historic kapok tree and fanciful sculptures.*

THIS PAGE *Now restored, the grand stairway's elegant Georgian balance and curves have been precisely preserved. The original pocket doors below the landing open to the loggia.*

ST. EDWARD CATHOLIC CHURCH

1998 Ballinger Award

St. Edward Catholic Church, designed by New York architect Mortimer D. Metcalfe, a graduate of Columbia University and the Beaux Arts Institute, is a stunning reflection of a New World interpretation of Spanish Colonial architecture. The church's history is illustrative of the will of the people to erect a place of worship in their winter haven.

Initially a Jesuit parish established in 1924, Father Felix Clarkson purchased three lots near the center of town in 1926 to build a mission church. Clarkson acted as both campaigner and general contractor, establishing a building fund campaign to encourage the burgeoning congregation to raise sixty percent of the total cost. Breaking ground on Easter Sunday of 1926, the church was completed nine months later, in time for Midnight Mass on Christmas Eve.

Metcalfe's original design for St. Edward employed a triple arched entrance with twisted Spanish Baroque columns, creating a complex that included a courtyard and parish house. A cloistered walkway and balustraded porch connect to the church. The principal structure is flanked by towers on either side; the southern tower is taller and dome-shaped, while the northern tower has a red clay barrel tile roof. Cast stone exterior walls, scored with stucco to mimic pointed vertically tooled stone, are a preview of the splendor found inside the church.

The interior of St. Edward is no less impressive. White Carrara marble and frescoed ceilings complement the vestibule and nave, separated by three walnut grilles. Over the grilles, the choir loft displays Bernini columns. The vaulted nave and arched stained glass windows are divided by marble pilasters capped by acanthus capitals. Upon opening, the church featured seventy-one handblown, painted pot metal glass windows, imported from Munich, Germany. Windows on the southern side depict the seven miracles of Jesus Christ, while the north side features depictions of Gospel parables. Sixteen arched clerestory stained glass windows, telling the story of sixteen major events in the life of the Virgin Mary, frame the interior's orientation toward the nave.

In 1995, the church's priest noticed large chunks of plaster falling from the ceiling and set out to repair the roof. The re-roofing project quickly turned into a two-year restoration. Deterioration was so severe that more than half of the scored stucco was replaced. Sagging foundations were secured with steel pin pilings. The south tower's dome was completely rebuilt, ornamental stonework on both towers was replaced, and code-compliant updates, such as railings and wheelchair ramps, were incorporated into the rehabilitation. Every interior detail was restored to its original glory, including intricate wood carvings and the barrel-vaulted ceiling with polygonal patterned painted plaster. The church's original windows were all repaired and resealed, maintaining their original Munich pictorial realism.

The church's namesake originated from Edward the Confessor, King of England from 1042–1065.

The church's main entrance is recognized in the Palm Beach Landmarks Designation Report as one of "the finest churches constructed in the early south Florida period of development."

The main façade is symmetrical with two towers balancing the triple-arched doorway.

OPPOSITE Metcalfe's design for the church cloister evokes a reflective, almost romantic ambiance. The simple cloister columns contrast with the monumentality of St. Edward Church viewed through the cloister arches.

HI-MOUNT ROAD HOUSE

1998 Ballinger Award

Hi-Mount Road House was designed by the talented yet lesser known Palm Beach architect Howard Major in 1939. Born in New York in 1882, Major was educated in architecture at Pratt Institute and the New York atelier of Henry Hornbostel of the Society of Beaux-Arts Architects. After practicing for years in New York and along the east coast, he came to Palm Beach in 1925. Originally working with Addison Mizner building Spanish style houses, Major came to believe the style was less than appropriate for Florida's subtropical climate. He is best known for popularizing the Bermuda architectural style during the 1930s. The Bermuda style is a West Indian adaptation of Georgian architecture, sometimes referred to as British Colonial. Major felt this style was a better reflection of American architectural history than the prevailing Mediterranean Revival style.

The house on Hi-Mount Road was designed for Horace Tucker, a relatively obscure freight agent for the Illinois Central Railroad. Finding a prime lakefront location, the architect set out to build a home that was simultaneously both modest and elegant. Asymmetrical in both form and fenestration, Hi-Mount Road House comprises a one-and-a-half story central block, with wings and additions extending westward. Approaching the entryway, one is welcomed into the home with a distinctive "welcoming arms" entry, a common feature in Bermuda style homes. Additional character defining features include a capped chimney and understated primary façade, as well as one of Major's signature embellishments, an octagonal window set within the façade.

Although minor changes to Hi-Mount Road House were undertaken over the years, the 1998 renovation of the house reinterpreted Major's original Bermuda style. The home's architectural style was enhanced with a trellised loggia, which joins the house with the lush gardens, while a series of open panels provide a light and shadow pattern. The dining room balances a sitting room on the other side of the loggia. Strategically placed beams obscure newly added air conditioning ducts.

Large additions to the north façade and back of the house increased the home's size by nearly one third. Respecting Major's original vision, every structural detail of the renovated home is designed to incorporate both form and function. The restoration of Hi-Mount Road House accomplished the renewal of what the owners called "a house of clouds" by combining Florida's Bermuda style architecture with an innovative new design fit for a contemporary lifestyle.

OPPOSITE *The traditional paneling of the library is lightened through the use of oak.*

ABOVE *A capped chimney illustrates one of Major's hallmark Bermuda style embellishments. The understated street façade retains a typical Bermuda style character.*

FLAGLER DRIVE HOUSE

1999 Ballinger Award

Flagler Drive House is emblematic of the affluence and elegance of the Boom Times in Palm Beach. Owned by the same family as Shaughnessy House, twin Ballinger Awards honored one family's dedication to faithful restoration. Designed by Marion Sims Wyeth in 1924, the house on Flagler Drive was built for Clara D. Frazier in a hybrid Mediterranean Revival-Neoclassical style. The builder, Cooper Lightbown, was not only a well-known builder in town, but also served as one of the Town of Palm Beach's earliest mayors.

Wyeth's trademark U-shaped design demonstrates his talent for integrating his architectural designs with the tropical setting through a patio or courtyard to, in his own words, "make the outside part of the house." Facing westward with a symmetrical façade and eight bays, the two-story house faces Flagler Drive, with the rear overlooking the Atlantic Ocean. The west-facing elevation features an arched wood paneled front door with decorative keystone surround. Its masonry foundation, hollow clay tiles, and stuccoed walls have two interior central chimneys capped with square chimney heads. Flagler Drive House has been modified several times, including enclosure of the open patio in 1962.

The award-winning rehabilitation of this magnificent home took over two years to complete. It moved an oceanfront pool to the west of the house, restored Wyeth's original patio design, and added classical balustrades to the patio and pool areas. Ornamentation was also added to the walls following the design of original applied cast stone embellishments. The remodeled interior allows the mass and volume of the living spaces to speak for themselves with simple forms and clear colors evocative of southern French styles.

Simple furniture and lighting in the remodeled living room emphasize the beachfront lifestyle, while arched windows, a coffered ceiling, and a stone fireplace create a powerful architectural setting, reflecting the room's original design. The award-winning rehabilitation successfully resolved some of the architectural contradictions introduced by a series of owners and alterations. Flagler Drive House demonstrates the ability to change the interior style of a house, while upholding the vision of the architect's original intent through thoughtful design.

The lacquered floors of the Florida room reflect the light streaming in from the French doors.

FOLLOWING PAGES *The ocean façade of the Flagler Drive home after restoration shows a simplified Spanish approach relying on elemental statements of repeating columns and a red barrel tile roof. The restoration design for the oceanfront veranda repeats the same strong horizontal balustrade found on the west side of the house and unifies the oceanfront with the courtyard.*

*Interior changes resulted in merging the
kitchen with a family breakfast room
decorated in vibrant colors.*

The color and style of the French Riviera are evident in the new kitchen at Flagler Drive House.

SHAUGHNESSY HOUSE

1999 Ballinger Award

The oceanfront Shaughnessy House is an exemplar of the ability of architects Marion Sims Wyeth and Frederic Rhinelander King to capture the gracious lifestyle for which Palm Beach is known. This Neoclassical style residence was constructed by prominent architectural firm Wyeth & King in 1938 for Jessie H. Shaughnessy, widow of Francis A. Shaughnessy, a philanthropist and the first president of First National Bank in Palm Beach.

The Shaughnessy family is known for their generous contributions to the Good Samaritan Hospital, one of the earliest hospitals in the region. A donation of $50,000 in honor of the late Mr. Shaughnessy provided the hospital with the funds to add a new wing to the hospital; the new wing was built by Wyeth & King. The subsequent owner of the Shaughnessy House was Edward F. Swenson, who served as vice president and trust investment officer at First National Bank. As a Yale graduate, Swenson was a member of Skull & Bones, Yale's "secret society" for the powerful elite. In 1964, the founder of a cosmetics empire purchased the home, which has been retained by the family.

Shaughnessy House, visible from nearly ten blocks away, is one of few extant Neoclassical style residences designed by Wyeth & King. Facing southward, this two-story house features seven bays and a symmetrical front façade. The front façade relies on Neoclassical-Georgian elements, such as a Greek style portico surmounted by a pediment with a fanlight. Four ionic columns lend the porch definition. The residence sits on a raised masonry foundation. A five-bay second-story balcony graces the west elevation, while two chimneys are located near the eastern side of the house.

The renovation of Shaughnessy House lasted over two years. The home's status as a historically designated property necessitated careful restoration of the exterior's appearance. The owners' love of history led them to preserve the interior plan, which was not required by landmarking, designed by talented Palm Beach interior designer Polly Jessup. Many of the home's decorative features and original furnishings were preserved, including an Empire couch in the restored entrance hall. The hall features an original checkerboard pattern tile, accented by a burst of sunflower yellow painted walls in lieu of its earlier greyish beige. The moldings and the arched doorways continue the Neoclassical theme down the hallway.

While architects like Mizner and Urban created dramatic masterpieces that inspired visitors with their elaborate detailing, Wyeth's inventory of accomplishments included many architectural styles that were responsive to changing social and economic conditions. In an interview, Wyeth indicated his preference for architecture that was not a "fad," but rather a natural evolution of Classical Greek and Roman styles into English Classical and American Colonial styles.

The formal dining room displays a reproduction of the original wallpaper recreated in a slightly different shade.

The front façade of the Shaughnessy House relies on Neoclassical-Georgian elements, including a Greek portico surmounted by a pediment with a fanlight. Four ionic columns define the porch.

RIGHT Classical ornament carries through to the ocean terrace with a foliated design for the balusters.

SOUTHSIDE

2000 Ballinger Award

The careful restoration of Southside created an opportunity to celebrate one of Palm Beach's lesser-known architects, Clarence Mack. A native of Cleveland, Mack opened an office in Palm Beach in 1935. Having extensively studied Renaissance architecture in Europe, Mack brought his talents back to the other side of the Atlantic and developed the beloved style, known as Regency, a tropical inspiration of the Neoclassical Revival style, which has long been a staple of Palm Beach's architectural heritage.

Originally named Southview for its lake view, the house now known as Southside was built in 1940 for Hugh Mercer Walker, a New York banker and vice president of the Equitable Trust Company, which was eventually acquired by what is now Chase National Bank. Walker had an impressive pedigree; he was a descendant of prominent American military generals dating back to the American Revolution.

Mack's classical details and symmetry followed classical principles of Ancient Greek and Roman structures, with influences from the Italian Renaissance. The original block of the north façade features seven bays with double-hung sash windows flanked by shutters on both stories, with scored stucco covering concrete block. The eye is drawn to the center bay, where the line of a parapet wall obscuring the roof is broken by a pediment. The south elevation's classical elements include roofline, door and window pediments, and loggias with Doric columns.

Southside's rehabilitation in the late 1990s nearly doubled the size of Mack's original structure while maintaining its classical proportions and detailing. It included numerous alterations and additions to the original house, including a garage addition and an extended new wing to the east that created a near mirror image of Southside's historic west wing. The original entry porch was replaced with a larger portico.

As the project evolved to meet the modern needs of the new owners, Mack's original understated detailing was replicated in the new additions, with strategic landscaping obscuring most of the new east wing. Southside is a splendid example of Palm Beach's Regency style. Its restoration created the opportunity to update a beautiful older house while also adapting Southside to accommodate modern lifestyles.

The vestibule is enhanced by whimsical pilasters crowned with palm fronds.

Southside's lakefront façade is unified by its strong horizontal massing. Yet the façade is never static, punctuated with rectangular and arched window groupings.

OPPOSITE *The dining room's architectural detailing maintains the symmetry and sense of scale evident throughout Southside.*

ABOVE *In the conservatory, part of the original house, a nine-foot ceiling was transformed into a vaulted ceiling.*

LAS PALMAS

2001 Ballinger Award

Las Palmas is a 1940 residence designed by John Volk, situated near the northern end of Palm Beach island. Broadway producer Sam Harris commissioned John Volk, who later designed the waterfront Royal Poinciana Plaza in the historic heart of Palm Beach, to build Las Palmas as a classical and elegant retreat. Harris' professional partnerships included George M. Cohan, Irving Berlin, the Marx Brothers, Cole Porter, Rodgers and Hammerstein, among many other names familiar to theater fans. He produced nearly twenty Broadway musicals, controlled seven Broadway theaters, and produced or co-produced American musical classics including "It's a Grand Old Flag" and "I'm A Yankee Doodle Dandy."

Known to the Harris family as Arabian on the Lake, the house known as Las Palmas boasts a spectacular lakefront location, now dotted with gorgeous palm trees that give the house its name. In sharp contrast to Harris' world of theatricality, Volk's Georgian style creation was markedly understated, a welcome respite from the hustle and bustle of New York City. Volk's timeless classic design flowed to the lakefront, where an upstairs loggia overlooks the water. A state-of-the-art swimming pool was added in the 1940s, which could be filled with salt water from the incoming tide in just thirty minutes.

Before its restoration, Las Palmas was shown as a "tear-down" house by realtors, but its purchasers saw its hidden beauty and decided to restore the home. In its first incarnation, Volk's Georgian design was complemented by Federal style interior elements, designed by Dorothy Hammerstein. This style was replaced by less formal decor and elegant chinoiserie pieces to provide a backdrop for the owners' Chinese Trade Painting collection. Old staff quarters, small bedrooms, and utility stairs were replaced with a large master suite on the second floor, which includes an exercise area, the master bedroom, and a beautiful walnut paneled library. The restoration team reframed walls and replaced windows, yet most significantly, the rehabilitation did not alter the original footprint of Las Palmas. In the restoration architect's own words, the "wonderful bones" of the house were preserved.

The story of Las Palmas illustrates the value in being able to look past a building's current state and recognize the potential in what it can become, especially when it is adapted to modern times while maintaining the integrity of the home's architectural history.

Las Palmas' front façade relies on balanced, classical organization. A half-balcony extends over the front door. The mass of the house is disguised by landscaping.

LEFT *The family room opens out to the pool and patio. The octagonal frames hold a collection of "sailors' valentines," a Nantucket tradition of shell plaques purchased by sailors for their loved ones at home.*

BELOW LEFT *The chandelier and hand painted mural add an elegance to the formal dining room.*

FOLLOWING PAGES *Palms and lush plantings frame the lake façade of Las Palmas. The ground floor loggia and second floor balcony create a transition between indoor and outdoor spaces.*

LAS CAMPANAS

2002 Ballinger Award

Las Campanas, or "the bells," has the distinction of being the first Ballinger Award winning home that began as part of a larger estate. Marion Sims Wyeth's design was originally joined to its neighbor to the east. In 1922, New York stockbroker Jay Carlisle commissioned Wyeth to build Las Campanas within an L-shaped subdivision overlooking the new Everglades Club golf course. The land was platted just a few years earlier by the Golf View Development Company, owned by Singer Manufacturing Company heir Paris Singer and New York stockbroker and financier E.F. Hutton. Wyeth was chosen to serve as the development company's first president.

Wyeth's entrance for Las Campanas was relatively modest in comparison to its Mediterranean Revival counterparts. Period lighting fixtures flank a carved stone door surround with the home's name carefully engraved below a coat of arms. A bell tower, lost when the building was subdivided, once crowned the east wing of the original house. Additions to Las Campanas were made in 1923 and 1927 to add a patio, swimming pool, terraced gardens, and loggias. Although known for his restrained style, Wyeth designed what has been referred to as one of the most dramatic living rooms in Palm Beach. Created from the original ballroom in 1927, the living room boasted twenty-eight-foot-high ceilings, cast stone trefoil windows with leaded glass, a fireplace, Venetian furniture, and an intricately painted ceiling.

In 1949, the estate was surveyed and the original house, including its extensive addition, was split into two separate homes. During this transition, the loggia wall was blocked in, marking the physical separation between the two houses. The house's bell tower, part of the original structure until its subdivision, became part of the adjacent home, leaving behind Las Campanas' namesake feature. Another unfortunate result of the split was a cramped, poorly lit stairwell. The modern-day rehabilitation transformed this space through the addition of a stairway tower accented with clerestory windows. Much of the project focused on increasing access and light within the house. While certain elements, like an additional door and trefoil arch to better connect the dining room to the loggia, were reimagined, certain aspects of the house, such as the paneled ceilings, required exact replication of original details.

The rehabilitation of Las Campanas after its purchase at the turn of the new millennium not only preserved the spirit of Wyeth's masterful work, but also addressed issues in need of modern solutions. Las Campanas is an expertly executed demonstration of the era's affluence during the Boom Times of the early twentieth century. Yet more importantly, the rehabilitation of Las Campanas demonstrates that an historic home can artfully reflect the spirit of the original design while meeting the needs of modernity.

The trefoil-arched windows of the family room are a distinguishing feature of the courtyard façade.

The dignified entry to Las Campanas, with its period lighting fixtures, conceals the importance of the interior spaces Wyeth created.

OPPOSITE *A delicate pattern creates a fanciful view through the iron door at the front of Las Campanas.*

LEFT *The formal dining room is decorated with a rock crystal chandelier and eighteenth century Italian mirrors.*

ABOVE *The living room rises to a spectacular height of twenty-eight feet. Its tall arched windows complete the impressive scale of the room.*

The wood paneled office creates
an intimate enclave within the
large estate.

RIGHT *The family room, which
opens to the courtyard, was decorated with a French antique
chandelier and Italian botanical
prints. The original painted
wood ceiling in the room
required only cleaning.*

CASA DE MIEL

2003 Ballinger Award

A decorative wrought iron gate leads to the southern entrance of the guest wing, originally the staff quarters.

Casa de Miel is a remarkable Mediterranean Revival home designed by John Volk and reimagined for modern life. Built for financier Frank Craig of Larchmont, New York, Casa de Miel quickly gained a reputation for its lively parties after its completion in 1927. The second owners were the Elmer Rich family, also known for their lavish evening events.

Known to the Craig family as El Retiro, the expansive estate features a large tower that rises from behind the asymmetrical front facade. The tower's brick veneer and decorative tiles sit in contrast to the stucco wood frame house and cast stone decorative details. The hipped roof is complemented by red clay barrel tiles and pecky cypress rafter tails.

Casa de Miel achieved landmark status from the Palm Beach Landmarks Preservation Commission in 1991 and was purchased two years later by those who would restore the home to its former grandeur. By this time, several subsequent modifications to Volk's design, as well as years of neglect, necessitated a well-thought out rehabilitation of the grand estate. One of the most striking aspects of this rehabilitation was the reconstruction of the bell tower, which was likely destroyed by the devastating 1928 hurricane.

Over the decades, the building was retrofitted with Mid-Century Modern elements such as jalousie windows and sliding glass doors that conflicted with the original design of the house. The rehabilitation removed the inconsistent replacement materials, and installed appropriate casement windows throughout the building, as well as decorative leaded glass windows framed by cast stone cinquefoil arches on the front façade. The addition of a new loggia and second story terrace with wrought iron railing overlooking the pool increased the outdoor living space. Complementing the architecture, the brick and coquina stone design of the main entry driveway brings the eye from the top of the main tower down to the street.

The restoration of Volk's early-twentieth-century design is demonstrated in its details. The Moorish inspired tower and belfry, decorative cast stone details, and fanciful wrought-iron adornments are indicative of the painstaking attention to detail required to restore a building that has endured additions, modifications, and neglect over the course of decades.

OPPOSITE *Casa de Miel is arranged in three distinct sections: the eastern section with a large tower, the central gable section with its decorative cast stone entryway, and a western section featuring the restored belfry.*

ABOVE *The restored decorative leaded glass windows provide light to the living room, highlighting the historic coffered ceiling.*

The new loggia sensitively increases
the indoor-outdoor living space.

RIGHT *From the pool, the reconstructed
tower's unique combination of brick and
decorative tile can be fully appreciated.*

WINDSONG

2004 Ballinger Award

Windsong is a Georgian Revival style home designed by John Volk. The sensitive rehabilitation of this classic Palm Beach home updated the house to complement modern living while retaining Volk's important architectural details. Windsong was built in 1939 for Ellsworth C. Warner, a business mogul from Minneapolis, Minnesota. The home was later sold to champion skier Ronald Bush Balcom and his wife Lulu, who was previously married to George Vanderbilt until his untimely death in the 1915 sinking of the British ocean liner *RMS Lusitania* by a German submarine. A later owner was George Meeham, a manager for the Ringling Brothers and Barnum & Bailey circus outfits, who spent many of his days at Windsong.

Located on a corner lot and situated at a forty-five-degree angle in the heart of Palm Beach, Volk's design for Windsong accentuates the use of natural light, utilizing the design of the house to take advantage of the views of Lake Worth. Windsong features iconic elements of Volk's Georgian Revival style: a symmetrical façade, hipped roof, and classical ornamentation. The distinctive portico features four columns and two pilasters with a simple acanthus leaf design at the capitals. The horizontal entablature features dentils and is topped with four matching finials. The decorative entryway is enhanced by the fanlight above the doorway.

The seven-month restoration of Windsong began by reopening a loggia that had been enclosed by previous owners. The reversion of the loggia to Volk's original plan returned the flow of light and the feeling of openness to the house. During the rehabilitation process, the restoration architect's team was vigilant in the protection of Volk's original architectural details such as the crown molding with bas-relief patterns, patterned friezes, and fireplace mantelpiece while adding new plumbing, electric, and air conditioning.

In the interior, the conversion of an ill proportioned second-story addition to a grand master suite returned the space to match Volk's original intention. A windowless office, devoid of natural light, was converted into guest bedrooms across from the master suite. The restoration architect also created a foyer around one of the home's two staircases, connecting it to a guest suite and replicating the original railings of the main staircase. The sensitive rehabilitation was praised for keeping Volk's original architectural features through the modernization of the building. A landmarked structure since 1990, Windsong's historic roots continue to grace Palm Beach while providing a modern living space for the twenty first century.

The railing on the staircase showcases a Greek key motif.

The distinctive portico features a denticulated entablature supported by columns with acanthus leaf capitals.

OPPOSITE *The classically proportioned gallery connects the public rooms of the home.*

An original marble fireplace is the focal point of the graciously sized living room.

OPPOSITE *The reopened loggia once again connects the indoor and outdoor living spaces.*

ABOVE *The unique siting of Windsong allows for breathtaking views of the lake at sunset.*

CASAROTA

2005 Ballinger Award

Relocation of the original entrance by Volk created a three-bay street-facing façade.

While Casarota is considered a John Volk design, its historic roots precede Volk by two decades. Designed and built in 1916 by early Palm Beach pioneer, master builder, and future mayor, Cooper Lightbown, Casarota was known as Eastways until the early twenty first century. Eastways began as a small two-story cottage owned by New England couple Emma and Manford Monroe. This cottage housed many families and underwent many additions in the early Boom Times of Palm Beach, but it wasn't until a generation later that the modest cottage was transformed into the Georgian Revival house it is today. Commissioned by then-owner Rudolph Horman in 1937, significant architectural and stylistic changes to the cottage were designed by Volk, whose reputation for creating impressive homes was well-established in Palm Beach by this time.

The Georgian Revival style, one of Volk's specialties, is still a popular architectural style today. Under Volk's design, Casarota's original front entryway was moved to the west façade to create a symmetrical two-story, three-bay street-facing façade. The new entry became accessible by two sets of steps leading to an arched paneled door framed by louvered shutters and a simple pediment. Volk's renovations expanded the living quarters by adding on to the back of the house an enlarged kitchen and loggia. The living room was also enlarged, through enclosure of the front porch, with a columned support beam defining the updated area. Other improvements included a bay window and fireplace in the living room, butler's pantry, kitchen, bar, vestibule, and a dressing room.

In 2001, the house was sold to a family that desired to restore Eastways to its Volk-era magnificence. This award-winning restoration is responsible for its current name, Casarota, which is Spanish for "broken house," as the family's children rechristened it during its rehabilitation. Careful to adhere to Volk's renovations decades later, the restoration architects left the exterior nearly intact, only replacing the double hung sash windows with impact windows. The interior rooms were opened up to create more spacious living and dining rooms, while upstairs the original five bedrooms became four. The back loggia was enclosed with French doors to maintain the indoor-outdoor connection and provide more square footage for the family. One of the most exciting moments of the rehabilitation was the discovery of the original Dade County Pine wood floors underneath the carpet and linoleum, which were preserved and restored.

LEFT *The floor plan of the house flows beautifully from one room to another.*

BELOW LEFT *Columns delineate the original front porch from the living room.*

RIGHT *The focal point of the kitchen is the Garland stove, a part of the home since the 1950s.*

BELOW RIGHT *Enclosure of the rear loggia created additional living space.*

JUNGLE ROAD HOUSE

2006 Ballinger Award

Jungle Road House was designed by the Swiss-born Maurice Fatio. This two-story Mediterranean Revival style house showcases the expertise required to restore the interior of a house in an historically sensitive manner.

Fatio is usually associated with large-scale residences, but Jungle Road House was built as a more modest, family-scaled house, reflecting Fatio's own tastes. The late 1920s marked a dramatic shift in the design and construction of buildings in Palm Beach for two reasons—the end of the Florida land boom and the effects of the devastating 1928 hurricane. This intimate house is believed to be the first residence designed by Fatio after his marriage to novelist and socialite Eleanor Chase. While it had been built on speculation, the newlyweds did live in it for a short period before it was sold, which was the custom of architects to do in that day.

The T-shaped building features a red clay barrel tile roof, arched doors, balconies, and a cast stone door surround. The entranceway is crowned by a petite window covered by a wrought-iron grille, with an adjoining series of windows accented by a stuccoed belt course below cast stone sills. In contrast to other Mediterranean Revival structures that mirrored Spanish and Moorish opulence, Jungle Road House featured simpler, more harmonious Italian influences, signaling the shifting mood in Palm Beach.

While the home's façade appeared much as it did in 1929, the splendor of the interior workmanship had faded over time. Using original architectural plans and historic photos, the owners of the house were able to restore Fatio's home to its former glory. The restoration architects worked hard to restore the home's refined original details that were stripped away from Jungle Road House. A crucial step in restoring Jungle Road House was reopening the loggia, which had been enclosed by a prior owner. The reopened loggia now boasts celadon-glazed walls, bringing the feeling of light and air to the space. Inappropriate changes by previous owners, such as the thick golden paint on the dining room mantel, were removed.

The extensive woodwork required for the restoration necessitated hiring a woodworker who could recreate the living room's milled pecky cypress paneling, an element removed by a previous owner. The dining room ceiling was restored with Italian Renaissance style vignettes painted with mythological and astrological themes on canvas and placed between the wooden beams. Fatio's Jungle Road House was designated as a locally significant landmark in 1996.

A close-up of the original staircase reveals weathered terra-cotta tile framed by wood stair nosing and rough-plastered walls stippled with a motted melon-colored glaze.

A rusticated Florentine doorway
distinguishes the entrance to the home.

RIGHT *Removed by a previous owner,
the room's original paneling was
carefully recreated using photographs
provided by Fatio's daughter.*

LEFT *Thick gold paint was stripped from the original mantelpiece revealing the intricate detailing.*

ABOVE *The orientation of the swimming pool was changed from north-south to east-west to enhance the vista from the loggia and terrace.*

MAGNOLIA HOUSE

2007 Ballinger Award

The marble flooring of the entry was restored to its original splendor.

The Magnolia House, designed by John Volk, was commissioned in 1939 by Palm Beach Modern Homes, Inc. The first residents were the family of Wisconsin realtor Ross M. Koen. Volk's restrained classicism for this home on the North End of the island was inspired by the fictional plantation home Tara featured in Gone with the Wind, released the same year.

In Volk's own words, "Families who have built winter homes in Palm Beach have been accustomed to living in traditional houses in the north…many wish to reestablish the intimate feeling of their northern homes." Therefore, he developed what he considered a house for "a planter who brought with him possessions from England." Magnolia House was designed in the Southern Colonial style, a variant on the Neoclassical Revival architectural style that followed classical architectural principles with Renaissance Italian influences popular during the antebellum era. The symmetrical two-story, four bay front façade is defined by its wrought iron balcony and two-story columns topped with acanthus leaves. Colonial style shutters frame its double-hung sash windows and French doors.

The restoration of Magnolia House rescued the spirit of Volk's original vision. The home was fortunate enough to avoid major alterations in the nearly seven decades since its erection, but the house was suffering from a damaged roof and decayed wood siding. Minor alterations included pragmatic changes like updating the electrical and plumbing systems, the replacement of asbestos roof shingles, and the addition of a patio and a pool. Intentionally focusing on restoring the building's essential design features, the amount of work needed on the exterior was less significant than the rehabilitation of the interior spaces. The first story's original wood and marble flooring was cleaned, restoring it to its condition in 1939. The second-floor layout was reconfigured for modern needs, adding en suite bathrooms to each of two guest rooms and a master suite.

Magnolia House, designated as a town landmark in 2014, was honored for the restoration architect's faithful preservation of the original structure, restoration of the interiors, and adaptation of the house to accommodate contemporary needs. It is an excellent lesson in the opportunity to rehabilitate and restore a home that has fallen into a state of disrepair, saving it from demolition due to neglect.

Inspired by the fictional Tara, the primary façade references the architecture of the antebellum period.

OPPOSITE

ABOVE *The addition of a porch and pool complements Florida living.*

BELOW *The large bay window offers natural light and views of the garden to the sitting room.*

VILLA EL SARMIENTO

2008 Ballinger Award

Now part of the Villa El Sarmiento estate, the home once known as Kenlewinai was built shortly after World War I by an unknown architect as a hybrid of a wood frame cottage. In 1931, architect Howard Major executed a massive renovation of the small cottage, transforming it into a British West Indies Colonial style home. Commissioned by United States Army Air Corps Sergeant James P. Kennedy of Minnesota, Major's renovation of Kenlewinai expanded the existing structure with an added veranda, an east facing arched loggia, as well as a second loggia on the west elevation. The western loggia features louvered shutters and a whitewashed brick chimney.

Major's architectural plan for the estate consisted of a symmetrical ocean facing façade with a loggia and second-floor porch. Textured stucco piers are crowned by molded capitals, while smooth stucco arches frame the recessed loggia. On the second floor, simple wood columns and louvers frame a five bay porch with three sets of French doors, providing views of the Atlantic Ocean. The primary entryway door features glass sidelights topped with an ornate fanlight. A porthole window in the chimney is embellished with a leaded teardrop design.

Several years after the 1998 purchase of Kenlewinai, the town's landmarking board approved a rehabilitation project, joining the property with El Sarmiento, the owner's adjacent estate. Major's house became a playhouse for the family's children and provided housing for staff. The renovation and merging of Kenlewinai with El Sarmiento created a thirty thousand square foot estate, nearly double the size of the original El Sarmiento. The Villa El Sarmiento estate is an outstanding representation of an historic house that was rescued from demolition and rehabilitated to suit modern lifestyles.

A porthole window with a teardrop design can be seen above the interior courtyard. The same window is repeated on the chimney located on the primary façade.

Major transformed a small wood frame cottage into the charming British West Indies estate seen today.

RIGHT *Modern interiors juxtapose the classical architecture of the exterior.*

EL CASTILLO

2009 Ballinger Award

The heavy wood entrance doors with decorative iron studs reinforce Mizner's reimagining of this Wyeth-designed residence as a medieval fortress.

The 1920 Mediterranean Revival style El Castillo was constructed by Marion Sims Wyeth as a modest Italian style home. The building was expanded several years later by Addison Mizner into a fanciful castle that dominates the surrounding streetscape. Leading steel magnate and Wall Street stock broker John F. Harris of Harris, Winthrop, and Company, commissioned the residence as a gift for his daughter.

Designed by Wyeth as an Italian Renaissance-influenced residence, El Castillo's massing began as two and three story rectangular blocks with hip and gable red clay barrel tile roofs, and white stucco-clad exterior. In 1927, Harris commissioned Addison Mizner to remodel the house, adding a crenellated medieval tower with window surrounds of cast stone, providing the centrally located El Castillo with views of both the Atlantic and Lake Worth. Mizner's cast stone battlements, heavy window moldings, and thick wooden door punctuated by iron studs added a medieval design to the house.

The 2007 rehabilitation of El Castillo was a substantial, two-year long project. The north-facing front door was cleaned and restored, with handles, hinges, and latches returned to their bright and vivid appearance. Several major changes included enlarging the original east-facing center window to accommodate a French door and allow the outside terrace to connect to the pool house. The original pool house and pool were restored. Paint was stripped away to return the pool house to its original cypress.

The most extensive area of new work on the house is both a restoration and a rehabilitation. The area behind the dining room, originally a butler's pantry, had been expanded over the decades into a working kitchen. After restoring the pantry to its original dimensions, the kitchen was moved into a seemingly new addition to the house that in actuality restored the home's original footprint. This kitchen now stands on the original location of the staff quarters, removed during a previous renovation. Features that could be saved were cleaned and restored, such as the original fountain. The living room ceiling was deemed structurally sound and its patina and imperfections preserved. El Castillo's rehabilitation is noteworthy and special, demonstrating the skill and vision required to respect the evolution of a home.

Wyeth's restrained design was expanded by Mizner through the addition of a five-story castle that included new living and dining rooms, a cloister, and courtyard.

The sensitive rehabilitation restored the original pool and stripped paint from the cypress walls of the pool house designed by Volk.

FOLLOWING PAGES *The living room's historic features were retained and restored, including the intricate stencil work on the beamed ceiling.*

The symmetry of the formal
dining room is accentuated
by the vaulted ceiling.

BELOW RIGHT *The kitchen
table is an original design from
Mizner Industries, Inc.*

OPPOSITE *The fourth floor
sitting room provides
spectacular views of the island.*

LA TONTERIA

2010 Ballinger Award

La Tonteria tells the story of a landmarked home that underwent extensive rehabilitation while retaining the features protected by the local landmark designation ordinance. John Volk designed the Neoclassical oceanfront house in 1935 for New York broker Colonel Edward J. S. Donovan. Later named La Tonteria, Spanish for "a foolish fantasy," it was the second house that Volk designed for the Donovan family. Donovan married speedboat pilot Grace Conners in 1933. Winning at least thirty regattas in New York, Florida, and Havana, Cuba, Conners sailed to victory in her twenty-six-foot vessel, "Miss Okeechobee," earning her international renown. In its heyday, La Tonteria saw its share of influential guests; the Donovan family hosted Secretary of Commerce Daniel C. Roper, United States Treasurer William A. Julian, Governor of Puerto Rico Robert H. Gore, Broadway star Myrtle Schaaf, and corporate titans of the day.

Close to the northern end of the island, La Tonteria was designed to cover an entire city block, adjacent to the former Kennedy Estate. Volk's design for the house is centered on a western-facing courtyard. The double-height Greek portico creates a grand entrance that dominates the façade of the two-story structure, an early example of Georgian style architecture in Palm Beach. Four columns raised up on high plinths support a pediment decorated with a central œil de bœuf, or "ox-eye" window. A double belt course divides the first and seconds floors, tying the entrance to the ocean block as it curves eastward.

The rehabilitation of La Tonteria, which took over three years, was a massive and costly undertaking, exceeding five times the original estimate. The restoration architects enlisted experienced artisans and craftsmen from Florida to Europe to ensure the historically accurate restoration of La Tonteria. Severe water damage discovered behind the exterior walls necessitated the recasting and waterproofing of every brick. The unique distressing chosen by John Volk decades earlier was recreated.

Rehabilitation of the interior was brilliantly executed to fit the owners' desire for a "relaxing and welcoming" home fit for a modern domicile. The study was doubled in size and the dining room exposed to more light from added windows on the east and west sides. Perhaps the most unique change made to La Tonteria was the magnificent stairwell—Volk's original counter-clockwise stairwell was reversed during the restoration. Nearly one third larger than its original size, La Tonteria's modern form includes an added north wing, changing its L-shaped footprint to its present U-shaped floor plan.

A new addition includes a pool cabana with trelliswork and a botanical theme.

The prominent ocean façade showcases
the home's Neoclassical features.

OPPOSITE The French walnut wood paneling adds warmth to the distinguished
study.

FOLLOWING PAGES Light from the east
and west windows in the dining room illuminates the chinoiserie-themed panels.
The height of the ceiling was raised one
foot to accommodate their large size.

LEFT *The double story portico epitomizes the monumental proportions of the Neoclassical style.*

BELOW LEFT *The loggia recalls the portico design of the entry in its classically proportioned arches.*

185

BATH AND TENNIS CLUB

2011 Ballinger Award

The Bath and Tennis Club, a Joseph Urban creation, is an historically designated landmark as well as an institution in Palm Beach. The Bath and Tennis Club was established in 1924 by New York financier E.F. Hutton and his wife, Post cereal heiress Marjorie Merriweather Post. When the club quickly outgrew its original facility, a new building was funded by club members and erected near the southern end of town in 1926. Urban's popularity among Palm Beach's younger crowd secured his position as lead architect on the new oceanfront Bath and Tennis Club, which officially opened on New Year's Day in 1927 to much fanfare.

Boasting a stucco exterior and a red barrel tile roof, the club incorporates rectilinear massing, and curvilinear shapes. Urban's 85,000 square-foot club was erected as a Mediterranean Revival building with Mission, Moorish, and Asian-influenced flavors. The original Mission style tower was lost in the disastrous 1928 hurricane and never reconstructed. Stenciled designs on beamed ceilings, leaded chandeliers, quarried keystone tile flooring, and ornate ironwork express these influences in the club's interior atmosphere.

The ballroom ceiling, inspired by the hull of a capsized ship, recalls the Providencia, a Spanish cargo ship that ran aground in 1878 off the coast of Palm Beach. The Providencia's cargo, twenty thousand coconuts, was salvaged and planted by locals. A decade later, coconut palms had sprung up all over the island, inspiring its name: Palm Beach.

Architect John Volk partially reconstructed the Bath and Tennis Club in 1947 after a disastrous hurricane inflicted widespread damage to the entire premises. During the three-month restoration and reconstruction, Volk rebuilt the club's ruined cabanas, added locker rooms, and enclosed the second-floor terrace in glass.

In 2008, the Bath and Tennis Club underwent a four-year restoration and rehabilitation, during which the restoration architects uncovered a few surprises. A Moorish deep-relief ceiling covered during Volk's reconstruction and expansion was revealed, showing Urban's eight-pointed star design. Due to the club's location on a ridge, the entrance is on the second floor, with the ground level providing beach access. While removing part of the roof over the landing, a window, long hidden behind stucco, was rediscovered. Both the ceiling design and the window were restored.

Modern-day elements were added throughout the club; air conditioning was added and a more efficient layout transformed the kitchen. The original fireplace on the south end of the ballroom was replicated on the north end, obscuring the kitchen and creating a more symmetrical feel to the room. Urban's original design for the living room was preserved. The condition of the ceiling was left untouched, protecting the patina acquired over nearly a century. A majority of the furniture in the living room dates to the club's establishment.

One of the first landmarked properties in the Town of Palm Beach, the exclusive Bath and Tennis Club is an outstanding example of combining preservation and rehabilitation techniques to modernize a non-residential structure on the island. The club's renewal echoes Urban's own words: "We recognize tradition, cherish and love it, but do not cling to it. We admire progress, strive for forceful expression, but shun sensationalism."

The crescent shape of the building complements Urban's theatrically inspired style. With this shape, the Atlantic ocean takes center stage.

OPPOSITE *Urban's iconic* rejas *decorate the upper story windows in the court-yard.*

OPPOSITE *Urban's eight-pointed star deep relief ceiling was rediscovered during the rehabilitation process.*

RIGHT *The rich hue of the walls enhances the original architectural elements and furnishings of the living room.*

BELOW RIGHT *The intrados of the restored arches have trompe-l'œil paintings of decorative tiles.*

LAGOMAR WEST

2012 Ballinger Award

Lagomar West tells the story of a portion of an historic subdivided estate in southern Palm Beach. By saving a portion of the estate, an early piece of Palm Beach's illustrious architectural heritage was preserved. The redesigning of the floor plan during the restoration enabled the slice of history to function as a proper home.

Designed by Addison Mizner for New York coal broker John Magee in 1924, the Mediterranean Revival sixteen-room Lagomar estate originally sat on six acres stretching from Lake Worth to the Atlantic Ocean. Two years later, the Lagomar estate was sold to Mrs. Henry Robinson Rea, heiress to the Robinson, Rea & Company fortune, a Pittsburgh iron foundry and machinery firm. At a party held in her honor in 1935, the wife of architect Marion Sims Wyeth sang "Stay as Sweet as You Are" to Mrs. Rae. Unfortunately, the post-World War II economy took its toll on Lagomar; after Mrs. Rae's death in 1951, the Lagomar estate was purchased by Alan M. Graf and subdivided into twelve lots, collectively named "Lagomar Park."

The award-winning Lagomar West house is but a small part of what was once a grand estate. The original residence, simply called Lagomar, featured an arched portico leading to a striking hallway with a staircase embellished with handrails of wrought iron. Other elegant touches included Woodite reproductions of Salamanca paneling, as well as an imported Spanish carved ceiling in an octagonal room. The original Lagomar also featured an impressive fifty-by-thirty-four-foot living room with a high, coffered ceiling and views of both the Atlantic and Lake Worth. The bedrooms, bathrooms, and a sitting room were located on the second floor. A ground level basement, located under the dining room wing, housed the kitchen and service areas. Staff housing and a laundry room were connected to the main house via a covered walkway.

Before the rehabilitation, Lagomar West did not have a proper entrance. The restoration architects addressed the issue by emphasizing movement and axial room relationships. Entering the property from the south, one notices the majestic house rising from behind the hedges, its clean lines and right-angles working together. Continuing around the hedges is the entrance and driveway. The design team ultimately determined that the home's exterior was to be viewed in a rotation upon approaching it, each of its floors cascading off the other. New ornamentation complements the remaining architectural elements designed by Mizner.

Rehabilitation of Mizner's second floor dining room allowed its conversion into a new living room. The project increased the lot coverage from 2,400 square feet to 4,500 square feet, expanding the total floor area from 5,900 to 9,600 square feet. The floor plan of Lagomar West now reflects the feeling of a New England townhouse. Described by both the owner and restoration architect as "a daunting task from all ends," the rehabilitation of Lagomar West commenced in 2007 and took just over two years. This magnificent preservation effort demonstrates creative solutions for a subdivided property.

The elegant spiral staircase connects the three floors in this section of the subdivided Lagomar estate.

LEFT *The original Mizner dining room, featuring woodite paneling, was transformed into the living room.*

BELOW LEFT *A glass table and lucite chairs juxtapose with the beamed ceiling and dark tiled floor.*

OPPOSITE *The courtyard is reminiscent of a Roman impluvium, a sunken courtyard designed to collect and carry away rainwater from the roof.*

The tiered symmetrical front façade pays homage to Mizner's design for the Lagomar estate.

RIGHT *Lagomar West, one of the twelve lots from the subdivided estate, combines Mizner's designs with modern amenities.*

VILLA ARTEMIS

2013 Ballinger Award

The 1929 Mediterranean Revival Villa Artemis tells the story of the preservation of a home built during an era of financial uncertainty. Despite the financial woes plunging the nation into the Great Depression, architect John Volk was able to execute a design that was both economical and architecturally stunning.

Originally known as Beaumere, and renamed Villa Artemis by its current owners, this residence was designed as a speculative house by Volk and his partner, Gustav A. Maass. Born in New Orleans, Maass was a graduate of the University of Pennsylvania School of Architecture and moved to Florida in 1921 to work at the architectural firm Harvey and Clarke. After designing several railroad stations in southern Florida, Maass formed a partnership with Volk. Together, they designed the American Red Cross building and redesigned the interior of First Presbyterian Church in West Palm Beach, just across Lake Worth from Palm Beach. Maass specialized in several architectural styles: Mediterranean Revival, Colonial Revival, Neoclassical, and Art Deco.

Vincent Bendix, an Indianan inventor and manufacturer who made his fortune patenting a drive gear that led to electric starters in automobiles, was forced to sell the residence just six months after its purchase due to the Great Depression. The home's second owner was Edward Albee Sr., owner of the Keith-Albee-Orpheum vaudeville theater circuit. The grandfather of prominent American playwright Edward Franklin Albee, the elder Albee had made a name in vaudevillian theater, touring with P.T. Barnum throughout the late nineteenth century. Albee was unable to enjoy the home for long. He passed suddenly the very next year in Palm Beach. Since Albee's death, the house has only changed hands twice.

In a subtle departure from Palm Beach's trademark Spanish-influenced architectural style, the home now known as Villa Artemis was designed as an Italianate villa. The home's sleek lines and more restrained decorative elements were reflective of Depression-era economic uncertainty. Two innovative elements reflected the creative tastes of the home's first owner. A tunnel leads from the house under Ocean Boulevard to the beach, one of the earliest in Palm Beach. Another less successful, but unique, feature in the residence was designed by Bendix himself—a car turntable for better access to the garage and driveway. Unfortunately, it did not function as expected and was quickly retired.

The rehabilitation and expansion of Villa Artemis created a contemporary feeling on the grounds of the estate. Primary concerns during the award-winning restoration were to increase and emphasize the flow of natural light, and to create a continuous flow between sections of the house. Pocket doors were installed between the loggia and the family room to offer privacy. Rehabilitation of the home included a second-story infill addition on the eastern side to expand the master suite. On the northern side, two powder rooms on the first floor and a closet on the second floor were expanded. The south elevation was extended approximately one hundred feet, and an addition on the west elevation created a new kitchen on the first floor, as well as a revamped bedroom, salon, and office on the second floor. The entire project increased the total square footage from fifteen thousand to just over eighteen thousand square feet.

The Italianate courtyard is complemented by bougainvillea and terracotta planters.

OPPOSITE *Lavender accents unify the interior design of the first floor living spaces.*

ABOVE *The living room's coffered ceiling is painted white to reflect natural light.*

*A new spare-lined pool centers
the patio overlooking the ocean.
The fireplace and lanterns add
to the ambiance.*

PELICAN HALL

2014 Ballinger Award

Pelican Hall was named after the custom bronze pelican sculptures that greet guests upon their arrival. The historically sensitive rehabilitation of Pelican Hall and impressive reuse of existing materials created a contemporary space that celebrates the architect's original intent. Historic elements of the house were restored, and a poorly executed addition by previous owners was reversed.

Pelican Hall was designed by Marion Sims Wyeth for R. Jay Flick, Jr. and his wife, Henrietta Ridgely Flick, in 1937. Originally from Pennsylvania, Mr. Flick had a diverse career—working first in journalism and publishing, then later moving to electric, gas, and light companies, and steel manufacturing. The second owner of Pelican Hall was Flick's grandson, Maryland realtor and liquor distributor Francis Warrington "Warry" Gillet, Jr.

The Colonial Revival style Pelican Hall is based on forms following design principles from the Georgian era. The primary façade is centered by a classically designed portico with a fan light above the entry door. Quoins distinguish the corners of the entrance bays from Pelican Hall's subsequent additions.

The fountain courtyard and driveway were designed in the late 1980s by renowned landscape architect Richard K. Webel, Sr. A principal of the firm Innocenti and Webel, he was famous for his designs at the Frick Collection and the American wing of the Metropolitan Museum of Art. His design for this home addressed challenges with the flow of traffic to create a grander sense of arrival to the property.

The key aspect of the restoration was the stairwell, which had been modified by previous owners. Unfortunately, the modification disrupted the flow of the house and needed to be reopened. By taking space from the garage to the north, the restoration architects were able to increase the width of the stairwell by four feet. Rectifying inadequate natural lighting has been a common theme in many restorations including this project. To increase light in the living room, the ceiling was lifted by six inches. On the second floor, a skylight was added to illuminate the dark space.

Custom bronze pelican sculptures frolic in the fountain, welcoming guests to this Colonial Revival estate.

The front entry hall and staircase were enlarged by four feet to provide a more gracious, contemporary space.

FOLLOWING PAGES The wallpaper in the living room was imported by the home-owner from a boutique in Paris.

LEFT *Looking back at the home from the pool, the sensitive additions to Wyeth's original footprint can be fully appreciated.*

ABOVE *The private garden's focal point is a modern sculpture by Julian Opie.*

PELICAN HOUSE

2015 Ballinger Award

Pelican House tells the story of the rehabilitation and stylistic enhancement of a mid-century residence within a planned community. This Clarence Mack Regency style residence is one of five speculative houses within a cohesive, landmarked neighborhood known as Regents Park, built in 1958. Mack was not only the architect, but also the builder, engineer, landscaper, interior designer, and real estate developer for the project. Built shortly before his retirement, Regents Park was one of Mack's crowning professional achievements.

Mack's development was intended to meet the demands of a post-World War II generation, a generation that was less focused on lavishly entertaining during the social season, and more concerned with the amenities required for a year-round residence. The first owner of the land on which Pelican House was built was the grandson of the founder of the *Chicago Tribune*, Chicagoan economist Alfred Cowles III. A graduate of Yale, he published a highly influential multi-year study on the perils of forecasting the stock market, which he coincidentally began two years before the stock market crash on October 29, 1929. He is also known for establishing the economic research institute known today as the Cowles Foundation.

The name Pelican House was inspired by the pelicans that land on the home's dock. It is constructed of wood frame with a hollow tile veneer sheathed in stucco. Regency style homes in Mack's development are characterized by high ceilings, tall windows and symmetrical axial floor plans. Mack's original design featured a triangular pediment over the front entrance, but he altered the design to avoid duplication with neighboring homes. Instead, Mack replaced the pediment with a portico, supported by simplified columns with Ionic capitals. Surrounding the central portico are five bays, each with sash windows and louvered shutters. The master suite and guest rooms are located on the first floor, with staff housing on the second floor. Forward-thinking features for the time such as ample closet space and built-in cabinetry compliment year-round lifestyles.

The owners of Pelican House set out to rehabilitate and create additions to the house that would blend with its neighbors in Regents Park. Additions included a loggia and two pergolas on either side of a new swimming pool. A pediment referencing Mack's original entryway design was added to the new western-facing loggia. Four decorative urns were added to the balustrade on the main façade, a typical embellishment of the Regency style. Replacing a wooden door capped with a transom window, the restoration architect added an arched iron and glass door to bring more light into the foyer.

Changes to the interior of Pelican House include exchanging marble flooring in the entryway for black and white checkerboard. A pre-existing skylight, a feature Mack employed frequently in his designs, illuminates the black and white patterned marble floor. Moving westward into the house, renovation of the living room included the addition of new moldings complementary to the existing woodwork.

LEFT *The new loggia references the triangular pediment Mack originally designed for the primary façade.*

ABOVE *Two pergolas flank the pool and frame the view of the lake and inland islands in the distance.*

CASA MARIUS

2016 Ballinger Award

Casa Marius is an Italian Romanesque style home designed by Maurice Fatio. This oceanfront two-story residence was built in 1928 for Wall Street banker Mortimer L. Schiff, a partner at the prestigious investment bank Kuhn, Loeb, & Company. Schiff was a well-known supporter of the Boy Scouts of America, faithfully serving as its vice-president for twenty-one years. He was elected as the president of the Boy Scouts in 1931, but passed only one month later. Schiff's daughter, Dorothy Schiff, was the owner and publisher of the *New York Post* for nearly forty years.

Originally called Casa Eleda, the home that Schiff commissioned by Fatio was named in honor of his wife, Adele. The word *Eleda* was her name spelled backwards. Keeping the tradition established by the home's original name, the current owners renamed the property Casa Marius, the Roman derivative of the owner's name. For many, the home is known as "the Ham-and-Cheese House." The name describes the distinctive banding of quarried keystone and brick unique to the house, complementing the warmth of the red clay barrel tile roof.

Fatio's inspiration for the house came from the villas near Siena, Italy. Centered around an internal courtyard characteristic of Italian palaces, almost every room connects to the outdoors. One-story elements flank two towers, creating a break in the massing. Intricately carved arches and engaged columns with capitals of varying patterns decorate the openings in the façade. Second-story windows line a belt course of floral medallions, and modillions of alternating gargoyles and acanthus leaves support the cornice.

The two-year restoration of Casa Marius achieved an unobstructed view of the ocean in the living room. The restoration plan called for one continuous piece of impact glass in each of six arched windows. Framing for the windows was hidden behind the columns separating each opening, allowing the glass to disappear, and drawing the eye directly to the turquoise waters of the Atlantic coast.

Original architectural details were preserved throughout the home while missing features were carefully reconstructed. Where original hardware was missing, new hardware was found that follows the same form as the original but differs from the old in a greater level of detailing. Exterior light fixtures, originally flanking the entrance were reconstructed to their original design through the use of old photographs.

On the exterior, years of dirt and mold were removed from the stonework, allowing the natural beauty and intricate detailing to be fully appreciated once again. In the courtyard, an original coral stone fountain was relocated and reduced in size to allow for a central open lawn. A new swimming pool was added to replace an oversized pool installed by an earlier owner.

The original coral stone fountain was reduced in size and relocated to provide more green space in the courtyard.

The estate's iconic quarried keystone and brick laid in a running bond pattern was inspired by the villas of the hill towns near Siena, Italy.

OPPOSITE
ABOVE *Carved coral stone is used for the fireplace surround and columns supporting the arched windows.*

BELOW *The pair of lamps on the sideboard inspired the color of the Venetian plaster and sumptuous fabrics.*

The original staff quarters were transformed into the family loggia.

*The main loggia retains important original
details, such as the stenciled ceiling, hand carved
columns, and a black pebble inlay on the floor.*

THE LIDO

2017 Ballinger Award

The restored marquee defines the entrance on the eastern façade.

The Lido is a Mediterranean Revival creation designed by the immensely talented yet largely unknown Miami architect August Geiger. Geiger was born in New Haven, Connecticut in 1887, the son of a manufacturer of moldings and fine wood-work. After graduating from Boardman's Manual Training School, he moved to Miami in 1905 and quickly became one of the leading architects in the area. The commissions Geiger received upon opening his Palm Beach office in 1915 illustrate how his reputation preceded him.

The Lido was commissioned by Bostonian entrepreneur Harry Kelsey, who founded Waldorf Systems, the third largest national restaurant chain at the time. After moving to Palm Beach in 1919, he purchased large tracts of land, quickly becoming the largest landowner in Palm Beach County. Kelsey is best known for the conception and development of the Town of Lake Park, originally named Kelsey City. The city plan was created by innovative urban planner John Nolen and the landscape architecture firm Olmstead Brothers. Although original plans do not exist, a 1919 Sanborn Fire Insurance Company map, used to calculate insurance premiums, indicates that construction of The Lido was underway prior to the issuance of the map in December of that year.

With the Lake Trail as the main thoroughfare during the time of construction, the primary elevation of The Lido faces the Lake Worth Lagoon. The west elevation is defined by the ornately detailed door surrounds of the north and south towers. Entablatures supported by pilasters depict a nature theme including birds and squirrels. A loggia connecting the two towers features twisted columns wrapped with grapevines. Over the years, The Lido underwent major alterations, including replacement of the original green roof tiles with red clay barrel tiles, and removal of the marquee above the entrance on the east elevation.

During the restoration, Ludovici tiles were installed to match Geiger's original design and the marquee reconstructed from historic photographs. A newly constructed open-air pavilion made of cypress features a hipped roof, also covered in matching green tiles. The original loggia was narrow, functioning more as an entry porch than an outdoor living space. The renovation nearly doubled the width of the loggia. A centrally located swimming pool was replaced with a new fountain framed by an allée of Royal Palm trees. These elements accentuate the loggia while two new pools reflect the towers on either side. The restoration of The Lido completely redesigned the grounds of the estate, taking advantage of the property's relationship to Lake Worth and complementing the home's symmetry.

The entrance hall is decorated with original millwork and paneling. The black and white tiles were reclaimed from a French chateau.

The Lido's interiors feel distinctly Victorian in comparison to the Mediterranean Revival interiors popularized by Mizner.

RIGHT The loggia on the western façade originally served as an entrance porch. The width was nearly doubled in size during the rehabilitation to create a proper outdoor living space. The new fireplace incorporates details from the grapevine-wrapped columns.

As seen from Lake Worth, the home is balanced by the north and south towers with ornate detailing. Twin reflecting pools mirror the symmetry of the residence.

CARSTAIRS HOUSE

2017 Ballinger Award

Carstairs House is an Addison Mizner designed residence built in 1923 and expanded in 1928 by Maurice Fatio. While Mizner never obtained a degree in architecture, he honed his craft in the offices of San Francisco architect Willis Polk, where he received training as a draftsman and learned the building trades. Carstairs House was commissioned by Daniel H. Carstairs of Philadelphia. Carstairs ran the family-owned distilling company Carstairs, McCall & Company.

Mizner's design for the Mediterranean Revival style Carstairs House embodies many of the characteristics associated with his trademark style. A distinguishing feature is the entry hallway on the eastern side with oversized doors inspired by what Mizner referred to as a "farmhouse of the Ferdinand and Isabella period." His fascination with Spanish architecture was cultivated by his time spent in Guatemala as a boy, while his father served as a diplomat in Central America. He was also influenced by his studies at the University of Salamanca in Spain. An asymmetrical façade, ornamental cast stone details, iron work, and both pointed and semi-circular arches are crowned by the red clay barrel tile roof. Mizner's unique interpretation of romantic detailing was expressed literally at Carstairs House in a heart motif on the wrought iron balustrades and window grilles.

In 1928, Maurice Fatio was commissioned to alter Carstairs House by its second owner. Fatio's design significantly expanded the footprint of the home, altering every elevation while maintaining the majority of Mizner's primary façade, with the exception of the heart motif which was omitted. Fatio's addition on the south side of the estate expanded the living and dining rooms, enlarged the master suite, doubled the number of guest rooms, and added a service wing with eleven small bedrooms for staff. He also added a beach cabana and oceanfront swimming pool.

Much like the modern restoration team that executed the award-winning three-and-a-half-year restoration of Carstairs House, Fatio largely preserved the character defining elements designed by Mizner while adapting the estate to the needs of the day. Updating the floor plan for a modern lifestyle was the focus of this latest project. Enclosing the motor court on the first floor created a family room off the kitchen. Fatio's breakfast porch was expanded to accommodate the owner's large family. The restoration architect designed a new staircase in the south addition, connecting the new family room to enlarged bedrooms in the former staff wing upstairs. Two Mizner windows removed by Fatio were restored in the process. Along North Ocean Boulevard, Fatio's wrought iron gates were carefully reconstructed from the original plans.

Mizner's lack of a complete formal education allowed him to envision his own whimsical creations without feeling the need to adhere to traditional period styles. The restoration of Mizner's work, filtered through Fatio's imagination, allowed the restoration architects to honor the genius of both men nearly a century later.

Enclosed by decorative wrought iron, the spiral staircase projects over the entrance hall and leads to the master bedroom.

FOLLOWING PAGES *Mizner's original design of a Ferdinand and Isabella period farmhouse was doubled in size by Maurice Fatio in 1929.*

LEFT *The scale of the living room is indicated by the large tapestry on the far wall and the stately carved china cabinet.*

BELOW LEFT *Original to the estate are the diamond shaped glazed tiles from Las Manos, a part of Mizner Industries.*

RIGHT *In the entryway, a set of six steps leads to the loggia. The pointed archway to the right leads to a whimsically located powder room.*

BELOW RIGHT *The original dining room was enlarged by Fatio through the addition of a third bay window, while still keeping in place the historic details of the ceiling and flooring.*

LEFT *The Mizner-designed pool is framed by original quarried keystone and anchored by four Sylvester palm trees.*

ABOVE *The dramatic effect of Mizner's entrance hall is best experienced when both sets of doors are opened, allowing for a continuous vista to the rear of the property.*

IVOR HOUSE

2018 Ballinger Award

Ivor House, designed by the firm Wyeth & King in 1937, is a British Colonial style residence constructed for the Joseph M. Cudahy family. Cudahy was born in Chicago, Illinois, in 1878 to Michael Cudahy, founder of the Armour-Cudahy Packing Company, one of the largest meat packing operations in the United States. As the heir to a cured meat packing business, it made perfect sense for the younger Cudahy to marry an heiress of the Morton Salt Company fortune, Jean Morton. Her mother, Joy Morton, founded the Chicago-based salt company in 1848.

Ivor House exemplifies Wyeth's mastery of classical architecture. The centrally located entry is highlighted with a portico supported by Doric columns. Dentils and a Palladian window motif add to the classical detailing. The entrance block is flanked by symmetrical wings featuring bay windows and quoining at the corners. A hipped roof and sash windows with shutters unify the façade.

Restoration and rehabilitation was a joint effort between the current and previous owners. The previous owners are credited with saving the building and commissioning a sensitive addition. The current owners continued preparation of the home for the future through reinforcement of the wood-frame and installation of impact windows. Integration of the latest technology illustrates how historic properties can be made more energy efficient through introduction of insulation and three-phase electric power. Clay tile floors and wood flooring throughout the home were restored. Original crown molding and paneling along with mirrors and French doors in the entrance halls were carefully preserved. A former porch on the second floor of the servant's wing was enclosed to create two guest bedrooms and with gracious en suite bathrooms. On the exterior, the balustrade was maintained to indicate the original location of the porch.

The current owners were deeply involved in the design and execution phases of the project with special attention given to the classically inspired landscaping and chinoiserie motif found throughout the property. Ivor House demonstrates the preservation principle that each owner serves as a temporary steward of an historic property. Each strives to thoughtfully adapt as needed and ensure perpetuation of the property.

LEFT *Renowned muralist Graham Rust decorated the walls of the long hall with native birds of Florida and Virginia, the owners' home state.*

BELOW LEFT *Scenes of a romanticized ancient China provide a neutral yet highly detailed backdrop for the colorful birds.*

RIGHT *Mirrored trelliswork reflects light from stacked pagodas treated as sconces flanking the original French doors.*

BELOW RIGHT *A newly constructed pagoda-style pool pavilion complements the chinoiserie motif found throughout the property.*

FOLLOWING PAGES *The masterfully designed additions respect the hierarchy of Wyeth's masterpiece.*

ABOUT THE ARCHITECTS

KENYON C. BOLTON, III 1943 to present
Kenyon C. Bolton, III is a direct descendant of the Palm Beach pioneer Bolton family. He is a member of the Board of Trustees at The American College of Greece. Since 2016, Bolton has been the Director Emeritus of The Cleveland Play House in Ohio. Established in 1972, his architectural firm, Kenyon C. Bolton III & Associates, Inc. is based out of Cambridge, Massachusetts.

MAURICE FATIO 1897–1943
Maurice Fatio was born in Geneva, Switzerland, and studied architecture under Karl Moser at the Zürich Polytechnic. After graduating in 1920, Fatio came to America and apprenticed with Harrie T. Lindeberg, a prominent New York architect of Norman and English style country houses. In 1921, Fatio formed a partnership with William A. Treanor. In 1923 they were asked to be the architects for the Olympia Beach development, now known as Jupiter Island. The following year Fatio opened an office in Palm Beach and moved into the Oasis Club. Fatio's many commissions for houses and commercial buildings in Palm Beach were based on his reputation in New York, as well as his charm, good looks, and European manner. In Florida, Fatio worked in many diverse styles, including Mediterranean Revival, Georgian, and British Colonial. The Reef, his Art Deco home in Palm Beach, earned a gold medal in 1937 at the Paris Exposition.

AUGUST GEIGER 1888–1968
Born in New Haven, Connecticut, August Geiger was the son of manufacturers of moldings and fine woodwork for interior décor. As the tenth registered architect in Florida, Geiger moved to Miami in 1905, where he established his own firm in 1911. He is most known for his Mediterranean Revival works, but was also proficient in Mission, Neo-Renaissance, and Art Deco architectural styles. In 1915, Geiger opened a second office in Palm Beach, where he was active until the 1940s. His most well-known works include Villa Serena, Homestead Public School, Miami City Hospital "The Alamo," Miami Beach Municipal Golf Course House, and St. Francis Hospital.

PHILIP HISS 1910–1988
Hiss was a partner in the New York architectural firm Hiss & Weekes. In 1925, the firm was commissioned to designed the new Bethesda-by-the-Sea Episcopal Church, bringing Hiss to Palm Beach. Hiss & Weekes did not establish an office in Palm Beach and did not pursue any other commissions on the island.

F. BURRALL HOFFMAN, JR. 1882–1980
Hoffman was born in New Orleans into a distinguished family, his pedigree documented as far back as 1657, when his ancestors immigrated to America from Sweden. Although Hoffman began his schooling in New Orleans, his parents sent him to Georgetown Preparatory at age eleven. He continued his education at Georgetown University and Harvard University. In 1907, Hoffman graduated with honors from the Ecole des Beaux-Arts in Paris, France. Best known for his connection to Miami's famous villa Vizcaya, Hoffman's career in Florida spanned over six decades and is considered one of Florida's most successful domestic architects.

JULIUS JACOBS 1901–1957
Jacobs was born in Pittsburg, Pennsylvania and moved to Lake Worth in 1918, working as a draftsman for G. Sherman Childs. After attaining his architecture license, he worked for Addison Mizner before he opened his own firm. Jacobs managed to master the European Renaissance philosophy, details, and design through self-study and foreign travel from which he developed his own distinctive style. He remained professionally active in Palm Beach from 1924–1942.

FREDERICK RHINELANDER KING 1887–1972
King was the co-founder of the New York City architectural firm Wyeth & King. Born in Rhode Island, King was a direct descendent of Peter Stuyvesant. After completing his studies at St. George's School in Newport, Rhode Island, King attended Harvard University, graduating in 1908. King served the United States during World War I in Paris, France, where his architectural horizons were further expanded. King served as a fellow of the American Institute of Architects and as the president of the Society Library of New York. He is best known for his work in New York City on the Episcopal Church of the Epiphany, and the Women's National Republican Club.

GUSTAV A. MAASS 1893–1964
Born in New Orleans, Maass was the child of German-American

immigrants. He received a degree in architecture from the University of Pennsylvania in 1917. Maass moved to West Palm Beach in 1921, working with the architectural firm Harvey & Clarke. During this period, Maass designed over twenty residences and offices throughout southern Florida, specializing in the Mediterranean Revival and Art Deco styles. Maass partnered with John L. Volk in 1927 until 1935, when he opened his own architectural firm. Maass' contributions to architecture in south Florida include residences, railway stations, and a variety of community buildings in the Fort Lauderdale and Palm Beach areas.

CLARENCE MACK 1889–1982

Mack moved to Palm Beach in 1935, during the Post-Depression era. Prior to his arrival, he built high-end houses in Ohio and Michigan. He received his Florida architectural license in 1936, and acted as both architect and contractor in his works. Mack became a developer, buying empty lots to build spec houses. In the 1940s, Mack decided he needed a signature style for his homes, and took inspiration from the English Regency style, building three of these homes in the estate section prior to his development of Regents Park and Parc Monceau.

HOWARD MAJOR 1883–1974

Born in New York City, Major was educated in architecture at Pratt Institute and the New York atelier of Henry Hornbostel of the Society of Beaux-Arts Architects. After practicing for years in New York and along the east coast, he came to Palm Beach in 1925. He soon became a critic of the popular Spanish styled homes he found on the island as failing to express an American "national character" as did Greek Revival architecture. In short time he determined the British Colonial, or West Indian, style as more appropriate for Florida. Even though he executed several Spanish style designs for some of his clients, a 1934 newspaper article titled "New Era for Palm Beach" gave Major credit as a pioneer in popularizing the West Indian design.

MORTIMER D. METCALFE 1880–1919

Metcalfe was born in Brooklyn, New York. He graduated from the Pratt Institute School of Architecture, then completed five years post-graduate work at the Beaux Arts Institute and Columbia University. Metcalfe began his architectural career in the offices of Hones & La Farge in New York City. In 1911, he became a member of the American Institute of Architects (AIA) and was bestowed the high honor of membership to the National Institute in Washington, DC. In Palm Beach he is noted for his design of St. Edward Catholic Church, and the Palm Beach Hotel.

ADDISON MIZNER 1872–1933

Addison Cairns Mizner, born in Benicia, California traveled the world (Central America, Spain, Alaska, Hawaii, Australia, China, Guatemala) seeing its architecture before arriving in Palm Beach. Mizner apprenticed in the San Francisco office of architect Willis Polk and practiced architecture in New York City and Long Island from 1906 to 1917. Paris Singer invited Addison Mizner to Palm Beach in 1918. Completion of the Everglades Club marked the beginning of Mizner's influence with the prominent winter residents of Palm Beach. His success in adapting the Spanish-Mediterranean Revival style to resort life brought a new era to South Florida. In 1925, Addison Mizner began development of Boca Raton. As city planner, his plans called for a complete Spanish city. He took responsibility for the layout of Boca Raton and the design of its important buildings utilizing the Mediterranean Revival style. Although he was backed by some of the nation's wealthiest men, Mizner went bankrupt during the real estate bust of the late 1920s.

JOSEPH URBAN 1872–1933

Born in Vienna, Austria, Urban trained as an architect. He was known for his theatrical design and his early illustrations of children's books. Urban immigrated to the United States in 1912 to become the art director of the Boston Opera Company. Two years later he moved to New York where he designed productions for the Ziegfeld Follies and the Metropolitan Opera. William Randolph Hearst was an important client and supporter. Most of Urban's architectural work in the United States has been demolished, with the exceptions of the Paramount Theatre and Mar-A-Lago in Palm Beach, Florida, and The New School and the base of The Hearst Tower in New York City.

JOHN L. VOLK 1901–1984

After working with the New York architectural firms of Friedlander and Knowles, and Watkins and Volk, John L. Volk came to Key West in 1925 to design several office buildings. The economic dislocations of a hurricane in 1926 and the collapse of the Florida boom led to his relocation to Palm Beach. In Palm Beach, he formed a partnership from 1927 to 1935 with Gustav A. Maass. In 1935 he started his own firm. As one of the most prolific architects in Palm Beach, Volk's work can be found throughout South Florida and the Bahamas. His notable commissions include The Museum of Fine Arts in St. Petersburg, the Parker Playhouse in Fort Lauderdale, and the original buildings for Paradise Island. In Palm Beach his early work was frequently in the Mediterranean Revival style, while later he helped popularized the British Colonial, Georgian, and other styles. The Royal Poinciana Plaza and Playhouse, the Beach Club, major sections of the First National Bank, and the arcade buildings to the east of the Everglades Club on Worth Avenue are among the many Volk buildings that survive in Palm Beach.

H. HOBART WEEKES 1867–1950

Weekes, of the New York architectural firm Hiss & Weekes, is best known for the Belnord, a Renaissance Revival style apartment building on the Upper West Side of Manhattan. Planned in 1908, the Belnord Apartments were advertised as the "largest building in the world," boasting nearly two hundred suites. Weekes served as treasurer of the Brooklyn Chapter of the American Institute of Architects.

MARION SIMS WYETH 1889–1982

Wyeth was born in New York City, the son of a prominent surgeon and political activist. He graduated from Princeton in 1910, spent four years in Paris at the Ecole des Beaux-Arts, and one year in Rome as secretary to the American Ambassador. When he arrived in Palm Beach in 1919, his first large commission was Good Samaritan Hospital in West Palm Beach, the first hospital in the county. The residences he designed in Palm Beach show a strong blend of Italian influences, especially in their courtyards and gardens. Later in his career he designed homes in a Southern Colonial style. Wyeth's houses can be found on almost every street in Palm Beach. His largest Palm Beach house was the residence for James F. Donahue. Among his other notable commissions are the Rectory of Bethesda-by-the-Sea Episcopal Church, the Florida Governor's Mansion in Tallahassee, the Norton Gallery of Art in West Palm Beach, and Doris Duke's Shangri-la in Hawaii. Wyeth was the first Palm Beach architect to be elected a Fellow of the American Institute of Architects.

PHOTOGRAPHY ACKNOWLEDGEMENTS

Palm Beach: An Architectural Heritage—Stories in Preservation and Architecture details the meticulous restorations of thirty-eight grand houses and public buildings in the exclusive resort town of Palm Beach. These structures were restored from 1988 to the present, and each has won the Preservation Foundation of Palm Beach's coveted Ballinger Award. The glorious photography showcased here respectfully documents the superb restoration of these architectural treasures, many of which have never before been published.

The Preservation Foundation would like to express its sincere appreciation to the following persons and organizations:

Robert T. Eigelberger
Flagler Museum Archives
Historical Society of Palm Beach County
Stephen Leek
Kim Sargent
Roberto Schezen/Esto
Alexandra Fatio Taylor
Mrs. John L. Volk

SELECTED BIBLIOGRAPHY

Aronson, Arnold. "Architect of Dreams: The Theatrical Vision of Joseph Urban." In *Architect of Dreams*. New York: Columbia University, 2000.

Ash, Jennifer. *Private Palm Beach: Tropical Style*. New York: Abbeville Press, Inc., 1992.

Bureau of Land Management. "A Self Study Guide: Legal Description and Land Status." December 2000.

Church of Bethesda-by-the-Sea. "A Tour Guide." 2009.

Church of Bethesda-by-the-Sea. "Restoration Report." 2011.

Curl, Donald W. *Mizner's Florida: American Resort Architecture*. New York: Architectural History Foundation, 1984.

Curl, Donald W. "The Florida Architecture of F. Burrall Hoffman Jr., 1882–1980." *Florida Historical Quarterly* 76, no. 4. (Spring, 1998).

CyArk & Partners. "Palm Beach Bath & Tennis Club." 6 July 2011.

De Holguin, Beatrice. *Tales of Palm Beach*. New York: Vantage Press, Inc., 1968.

DeVries, Janet. *Sport Fishing in Palm Beach County: Images of America: Florida*. Charleston, SC: Arcadia Publishing, 2008.

Dunlop, Beth. "Designers Keith Irvine and Jason Bell Put a Fresh Spin on Palm Beach Traditional." *House & Garden*. December 2003.

Earl, Polly Anne and the Preservation Foundation of Palm Beach. *Palm Beach: An Architectural Legacy*. New York: Rizzoli International Publications, Inc., 2002.

Fatio, Alexandra. *Maurice Fatio: Architect*. Stuart, FL: Southeastern Printing, 1992.

Garden Club of Palm Beach. "House and Garden Day."

Garden Club of Palm Beach. *The Plan of Palm Beach*. 1930.

Geisler, F.E. (photographer). *Palm Beach Villas: Volume II*. Palm Beach, FL: Davies Publishing Co., c. 1934.

Gill, John Freeman. "A House Divided." *Avenue Magazine*. 13 January 2017.

Harris, Cyril M., ed. *Illustrated Dictionary of Historic Architecture*. New York: Dover Publications, Inc., 1977.

Historical Society of Palm Beach County. "Palm Beach County History Online."

Hoffstot, Barbara D. *Landmark Architecture of Palm Beach*. Pittsburgh, PA: The Walden Trust, 1991.

Hyde, Charles K. *Storied Independent Automakers: Nash, Hudson, and American Motors*. Detroit: Wayne State University Press, 2009.

Johnston, Shirley. *Palm Beach Houses*. New York: Rizzoli International Publications, Inc., 1991.

Koskoff, Sharon. *Art Deco of the Palm Beaches*. Charleston, SC: Arcadia, 2007.

Luxury Florida Homes. "Casa della Porta: A Palm Beach Landmark…A Palm Beach Masterpiece." Vol. 11/5. n.d.

Marconi, Richard A. *Then & Now: Palm Beach*. Charleston, SC: Arcadia Publishing, 2013.

Mark, Rebecca and Rob Vaughan, eds. *The South: The Greenwood Encyclopedia of American Regional Cultures*. Westport, CT: Greenwood Press, 2004.

Mayhew, Augustus. "America First: Howard Major at Palm Beach." *New York Social Diary*. 12 January 2017.

Mayhew, Augustus. *Lost in Wonderland: Reflections on Palm Beach*. West Palm Beach, FL: Palm Beach Editorial Services, 2012.

Morris, Charles R. *The Tycoons: How Andrew Carnegie, John D. Rockefeller, Jay Gould, and J.P. Morgan Invented the American Supereconomy*. New York: Henry Holt and Company, LLC, 2005.

Murray, Nancy. *Restoring the Magic: Bath & Tennis Club 2008–2011*. Lake Worth, FL: M. R. Publishing, Inc., 2012.

New York Social Diary. "The End of the Last Long Weekend." 2 September 2013.

Notes on the Architect of the Willard Home: Maurice Fatio. Hobe Sound Tour, 31 January 1978 [Author unknown].

Palm Beach Homes. "Casa della Porta Opens the Door to Ballinger Award." 11–17 December 1993.

Palm Beach Today. December 1993.

Pederson, Ginger L. and Janet M. Devries. *Pioneering Palm Beach: The Deweys and the South Florida Frontier*. Charleston, SC: The History Press, 2012.

Silvin, Richard René. *Villa Mizner: The House that Changed Palm Beach*. West Palm Beach, FL: Stargroup International. 2014.

Social Register Association. 1937 *Social Register*. 1938.

Solly, John. "Southward Ho!" in *Motorboating: The Yachtsmen's Magazine* 73(5). May 1944.

Southern Methodist University. "Henry Robinson Rea's 'Lagomar' Estate Palm Beach, FL." *Robert Yarnall Richie Photograph Collection.* Description by Mockler, Kim. Image Credit: Richie, Robert Yarnall. 22 January 1933.

Spencer, Wilma Bell. *Palm Beach: A Century of Heritage.* Washington, DC: Mount Vernon Publishing Co., Inc., 1975.

St. Edward Catholic Church. 75 Years: 1926–2001.

Tolf, Robert and William Olendorf. *Addison Mizner: Architect to the Affluent.* Fort Lauderdale, FL: Gale Graphics, 1983.

United States v. American Can Company et. al. U.S. District Court, D. Maryland. 230 F. 859. 23 February 1916.

University of Michigan. *The Inland Architect and News Record* 9(1). February 1887.

Volk, Lillian Jane, Lory Armstrong Volk, & William Dale Waters. *John L. Volk: Palm Beach Architect.* Palm Beach, FL: John L. Volk Foundation, Inc., 2001.

Warner et al. v. Florida Bank & Trust Co. at West Palm Beach et al. Circuit Court of Appeals, Fifth Circuit. No. 11733. 160 F.2d 766. 10 April 1947.

NEWSPAPERS
The Baltimore Sun
Berkeley Daily Gazette
Cincinnati Enquirer
Des Moines Register
The Madison Eagle
New York Clipper
Ocala Banner
Palm Beach Daily News
Palm Beach Post
The Tampa Times
The Scranton Republican
Wall Street Journal

TOWN OF PALM BEACH RECORDS
Architectural Commission Minutes
Planning & Zoning Commission Minutes
Landmarks Preservation Designation Reports
Town Council Meeting Agendas

INDEX